PRAISE FOR 'TWEETS FROM THE TRE

'POTENTLY HUMAN AND UPLIFTING'
'A post-modern collage of poetry, tweets, historical documents, and photographs, this dances through the scarred landscape that exists between World War 1 and the present to create a moving impression of "The Great War" and its lingering effects on current generations. Carmichael renders the horror and the heartbreak of this conflict in a creative and deeply personal way, exploring the stories of the heroes—both sung and unsung—the soldiers, the nurses, and the families who bore the weight of the traumatized vets' behaviours when they came home. Like all good art, this book is potently human and uplifting, at once a grim testament to what we are capable of inflicting and a celebration of what we can endure.
— DEREK HANEBURY, AUTHOR/NOCTURNAL TONGLEN

'A REMARKABLE VOICE ... EXCEPTIONAL POWER & EMOTION'
'In TWEETS FROM THE TRENCHES, author Jacqueline Carmichael presents a marvellously inventive look at the First World War experiences of her grandfather ... A remarkable voice from 100 years ago speaking to us today with exceptional power and emotion. "I look like a loose button on an overcoat," says Black Jack after four years of war. "Most of the boys I came with are gone." His words are at times mingled with those of the author who displays her own poetic talents as she explores the impact of the war on Black Jack and his family. '
— GRAHAM THOMSON, COLUMNIST/EDMONTON JOURNAL

'ACCESSIBLE FOR GENERATIONS'
'"Lest we forget" takes on an entirely different meaning on the pages of Jacqueline Carmichael's wonderful new book. The images that she invokes through these poems, songs, images and tweets make the war to end all wars accessible for generations far removed from its carnage or from the lessons that have yet to be learned one hundred years later.'
— GORD JOHNS, MEMBER OF PARLIAMENT/COURTENAY-ALBERNI

'BRILLIANT BODY OF WORK, POETIC & BEAUTIFUL AMIDST RUIN'
'A visceral account of the horrors of war and the fighting that continues within a soldier long after the battles are won and lost. A sobering and lyrical depiction of war and trauma. She conveys the very essence of catastrophe: war and the impossible task soldiers face in ridding themselves of its horror. A brilliant body of work, poetic and beautiful amidst ruin.'
— EMILY OLSEN, FOUNDER/THE CONNECTION PROJECT

'CAPTIVATING STORY'
'Captures the sounds, sights and feelings of war ... amazingly descriptive.'
— BILL CHAPMAN/COALDALE, ALBERTA

'BRIMMING WITH VIBRANCY'
'Tweets From the Trenches by J.L. Carmichael is a genre-bending look at one of the most significant periods of world history. In this project, Carmichael is in communication with one of the newest forms of communication -- social media -- yet is firmly rooted in the oldest form of communication -- the splendour of poetry. It's an innovative mind that can re-think such possibilities for history, and Carmichael's is a project brimming with vibrancy.'
— WAYDE COMPTON, THE WRITERS STUDIO, SIMON FRASER UNIVERSITY

'A BOOK AND A JOURNEY'
'Carmichael has spent years dissecting, digesting, curating and puzzling over the journals of George Anderson "Black Jack" Vowel. With this book, she offers a touching treatise of what she learned from about how we communicate and how we tell stories and how the telling shapes the way we remember. She writes: "Smell the TNT / Hear the whistle of the shell's arc / Feel the panic slip in the mud underfoot / Hashtag that." This is a book and it is a journey. It is carefully crafted with the feel of white archive gloves and parchment and tweezers, but the urgency of the writing and the creativity of the hybrid text lifts the stories out of the yellowed pages of history and right into your social media feed.'
— AUTUMN PHILLIPS, THE CHARLESTON POST & COURIER

'FAST-PACED ... POETRY PAIRED WITH JOURNALISM'
'Carmichael takes the war to end all wars and places it in a world of tweets and instant fast-paced feedback pulling the past into the present ... She reminds us that war continues in an everlasting loop of trenches and guns and boys fighting Fritz while cell phones are imagined but "set on silent when they slip over the top lest a sniper hear & hone in on their heart." Carmichael sits in Vimy trenches and tweets from an account in her grandfather's name. This is a kind of poetry paired with journalism. History with metaphor. Technology set in a real world we barely can imagine now. Thankfully, Carmichael can and we follow her, with curiosity and awe, into that bloody past, learn of women who hid their identities so they could fight, men who hid their fighting so they could continue to live.'
— YVONNE BLOMER, CITY OF VICTORIA POET LAUREATE/AUTHOR/SUGAR RIDE

'AN ASTONISHING BOOK ... FINELY-CRAFTED ... A MUST READ'
Dip into this astonishing book to find a generation of Canadian soldiers, nurses and families who were part of WW1. Through vivid imagery, first-hand accounts and photographs, Jacqueline Carmichael tells of the hard flint of death, and gives the reader a keener appreciation for the simple echo of mortal moments. This finely crafted collection of poems is a tribute to her grandfather, finally encompassing humanity in its too familiar refrain. A must read for us all in these days of doubt and uncertainty
— JUDE NEALE, AUTHOR/SPLENDID IN ITS SILENCE

'REMARKABLE STORYTELLING!'
One of my favourite reads of the 2000s. An inspirational, innovative work that will resonate with readers across all generations. The clever format makes for a brisk read, yet the poignant imagery compels you to double back to appreciate the complexity. Remarkable storytelling!
— PHILIP WOLF/VANCOUVER ISLAND FREE DAILY NEWS

TWEETS
FROM THE
TRENCHES

Little True Stories of Life & Death

on the Western Front

JACQUELINE CARMICHAEL

Special thanks to CanadianLetters.ca for select excerpts & images in this book.

ISBN: 9781718021464

Carmichael, Jacqueline 1961-

   Tweets From The Trenches: Little True Stories of Life & Death on the Western Front/ by Jacqueline Carmichael

Cover photo Steven Van Den Eynde: Canada Bereft overlooks the Douai Plain, at Vimy Canadian National Memorial

Book design Jacqueline Carmichael/Brad K. Larson

Every effort has been made to fulfill requirements in regard to reproducing copyright material. The author will gladly rectify any omissions soon as possible.
For information about permission to reproduce selections from this book, or for information about special discounts for bulk purchases/educational discounts, contact Carmichael.jacqueline@gmail.com

www.tweetsfromthetrenches.com

PREFACE

The trench letters of my paternal grandfather, Oklahoma and Alberta farmer George "Black Jack" Vowel, were turned into a radio piece on CBC years ago, & then returned to the family by the daughter of Louisa "Bebe" Watson Small Peat, who corresponded Black Jack in the Great War and kept his letters. She & her husband, war hero Harold Peat, included Black Jack in their wartime books, *Private Peat* & *Mrs. Private Peat*. Transcribing those letters, & Black Jack's journals, started me on a research odyssey. The *Tweets from the Trenches: Little True Stories of Love & Death on the Western Front* project started with a social media experiment on Twitter & Facebook as I envisioned my grandfather, @BlackJackVowel or #AlbertaWorldWarISoldier, "hunkered down under a hunk of tin" amidst pouring rain and artillery fire, desperately trying to be safe, while using a smartphone to communicate with loved ones a world away. Articles and media attention about that experiment — & walking on Europe's Western Front in their bootprints in 2016 & 2017 — eventually lead to this hybrid literary project, written in what I consider "flash documentary creative non-fiction." I have generally labelled pieces drawn specifically from his journals with "BLACK JACK" at the beginning of the title, and have italicized his words within those pieces.

My research broadened as I read hundreds of letters & journals from others like him. I have included some larger excerpts from letters & memoirs, giving them proper credit & a "drop cap" treatment (large first letter) to help distinguish them. There are so many stories ... millions of them. This is a tiny sampling. As inclusive as possible, but by no means exhaustive. The material is generally organized along a year-by-year timeline, with years as chapter headers. I make no claim to the studied skills of professional battlefield guides and history experts. I'm just a writer telling stories to understand the past in my own eclectic way.

- *Jacqueline Carmichael*

@BLACKJACK VOWEL

**FOLLOW ALBERTA
WWI SOLDIER
#LESTWEFORGET**

Delivering rations to the front/
dodging bullets & mortar fire both
Bullets ripped the dirt up all round me
but none of them were marked Black Jack

- *George Anderson "Black Jack" Vowel*

CONTENTS

#1917   51

#1918

#1914

28 June 1914:

Austrian Archduke Franz Ferdinand & wife Sophie assassinated in Sarajevo by Serbian nationalists. Nations begin lining up behind the world's top economic powers: the Triple Entente powers are based on France/Russia/the United Kingdom of Great Britain & Ireland, & the Central Powers are Germany & Austria-Hungary.

28 July 1914: Austria declares war on Serbia. Russia sided with Serbia, Germany declares war on Russia & France, invading neutral Belgium on its way to invade France.

4 Aug. 1914:

Great Britain declares war on Germany. Canada is automatically at war too.

22 Aug 1914:

War Measures Act passes.

1 Oct 1914:

First Canadian Division sails for Britain.

October – November 1914:

First Battle of Ypres (in Belgium.)

Germany fails to reach English Channel.

1 Nov 1914:

Four Canadians killed with the sinking of the HMS Goodhope

in the Battle of Coronel off Chile are the first Canadians killed in action.

From 1914-1917

Two opposing armies will be basically deadlocked

on the 600-mile Western Front in the trenches of Belgium & France.

PLEASE MR. POSTMAN

Billions sent
A thin barbed wire of connection running through them
Little papery bits of war /Thin slices of Front life
scrawled in corners of dugouts under skies brooding rain
Concentration disrupted by strafing bullets
Dirt spattered by shell explosions
Trench existence splayed on pages
Ripped from journals & folded hastily
The original "twitter" - stuffed into a tiny canister
strapped to a pigeon leg/
wafted on wings to a safe loft
Or addressed to a world away
Postmarked "Feed the Guns with War Bonds"
{even on 18 Nov 1918/a week after Armistice}
Tied in bundles/crates stowed
in the bellies of ships/dodging u-boats
Shuttled on rails/in jalopies
Tucked into cast-iron mail boxes in Musquodoboit & Calgary
Tipped into brass door slots in Komoka & Milwaukee
Floating down to the floor in St. John's & Tulsa & Rhotenburg
to wood floors in Neepawa & wool carpets in Moose Jaw & Brooklyn
Left on quarter-sawn oak entry tables
in Westaskiwin & Wassau & Woonsocket
Seized with fervor in Kamloops & in Edinburgh/
by fathers & mothers in Brandon & New Orleans
& Casablanca & Walla Walla & Mermansk
brothers & sweethearts in Charlottetown &
Yorkshire & Beijing & Berlin
Opened with surgical delicacy
in Trois Rivieres & Three Rivers & Florence
lest one drop spill [1]

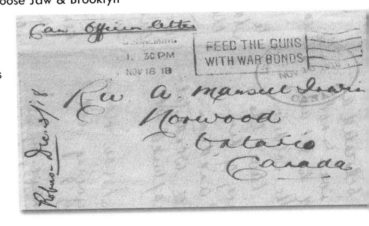

---

[1] According to the United Kingdom's Royal Mail, 19,000 mail bags crossed the English Channel every day in 1917. The Royal Mail's Home Depot was handling 12 million letters and a million parcels at its wartime peak. An estimated two billion letters were addressed to or from servicemen during the war. PHOTO: Envelope with postmark "FEED THE GUNS WITH WAR BONDS" courtesy CanadianLetters.ca

MY WESTERN FRONT/MY GRANDFATHER

My family has genetic roots on the Western Front: French/German/Belgian
My two grandfathers/one American/one Canadian
They each signed up for "the Great War" soon as they could
Both were in the trenches/ for "the whole thing"/both surviving/but with different outcomes
So after transcribing journals & letters I went there too
Stepped into sepia tones/like walking into an old photo album
At Ypres (leper) & Vimy Ridge I walk where they marched
Crouching in trenches where they dodged shells

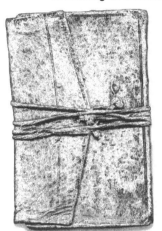

But with none of the panic they felt
Here he dodged bullets sent over by Germans {codename "Fritz"}
Here shrapnel rained down
And on the grand steps of
the Canadian memorial at Vimy Ridge
faint echoes of shelling are stilled by my keyboard's clack-clacks
New digital boots in old analog footprints/
feet strangely cold & wet
I wanted to know what insidious germ
squatting on DNA / what artifact brought home in his trunk/
What unexploded psychic mortars lurked behind that rusted latch
What hardships shaped/misshaped those who came after
I wrote hybrid poetry with their ghosts

A sort of flash documentary creative non-fiction prose
Stories from Commonwealth-side participants
Mesmerizing letters & journals/the social media posts of their day/
at a time that was equal parts boredom & deprivation/
but often sheer/horrific carnage/chaos

Journalistic long-form instincts
yield to the demands of
shortened attention spans/
including mine
Succinct retweets/poems/haiku
After all/there are those three
powerful words/
just three it boiled down to:
LEST. WE. FORGET.

Smartphone image/Pixabay

3

THE TWITTER PROJECT

. **alberta wwi soldier** @blackjackvowel **1** year reunion: came away/ couldn't stand to hear boys talk **of poor devils with us year ago/absent now.** #poppy #wwi #legion #blackjack

. **alberta wwi soldier** @blackjackvowel 1st anniversary of going to trenches. reunion at ymca, not **many old fellows left** #poppy #wwi #yeg #yyc #legion #blackjack #ableg #remember

. **alberta wwi soldier** @blackjackvowel , france: battleground of souche, labyrinthe where french lost so many. thousands lie there yet #blackjack #wwi #legion

. **alberta wwi soldier** @blackjackvowel 1915 germans sent over 10,000 shells in hour & half. so damn homesick i can hardly do any work. #blackjack #remember#ww1 #ableg #veterans

What would the war have been like if a soldier had a #Smartphone a century ago? An ace might get a ticket for texting while flying /A doughboy might use GPS for get across No Man's Land/ Lads would snap selfies with shells literally photobombing their pics

Drones could snap aerial photos of enemy territory — wait, this was a thing/In 1908 Julius Newbronner invented an analog hack - a tiny camera like a little GoPro to strap to pigeon chests!

I give my long-gone @grandfather's ghost a social media presence & tweet excerpts from his #journals & letters as if I were Alberta WWI Soldier (@BlackJackVowel)

He reaches out from beyond the grave attracting Twitter followers/Facebook friends/

Edmonton Sun social media columnist Linda Hoang reports on him/Papers write about him

Three generations follow my dead grandpa's social media outbursts half a century after a tractor pinned him to the dirt of his Peace River farm, sending him to his grave before we could ever meet

It's long overdue/this 15 minutes for George Anderson "Black Jack" Vowel & his trenchmates/

We will retweet them

PHOTO left: The original Steampunk — in this WWI era picture, pigeon with a camera used for aerial photos. Courtesy Bundesarchiv Bild.

Smartphone image/Pixabay

POSTCARDS FROM THE EDGE OF THE ABYSS

This was how they Tweeted/Their grapevine:
A postcard trundled across continents/oceans
into a cast-iron mailbox was just a slow Tweet
Their Smartphone? Pen, paper, thin envelope,
a canceled stamp hanging on for dear life
through onioned layers of handling
Instead of a drop-down menu of "who should see this"
it was posted/censored/delivered/pressed in a
scrapbook/ shown over tea/at the market
No Facebook post but a journal entry/
Not a text but a postcard of a cathedral:
"Look Ma I'm in Cologne"
No meme/but a propaganda poster to influence/persuade
Bad news? Not a voicemail but a telegram/
crumpled in distress/abandoned damp on a hall table
or the dreaded sorry-to-inform-you knock on the door
If he was gone, a photo on the mantle instead of a selfie on Instagram/
& no Go Fund Me for the widow & his children[2]
    Those messages are still out there/blinking their way to us
      Like stars emitting light left from explosions eons past
        We are all of us tagged in those posts

---

[2] PHOTO by Daphne Vangheluwe: Social media captures the solemnness of the Last Post at the Menin Gate in Ieper, Belgium/Mail courtesy CanadianLetters.ca.

THE SOCIALMEDIASPHERE THEN

They're out there still
wherever old messages go
Terse scribbles from World War I
as if farmboys/doughboys
/flyboys/nurses
clawed Smart phones hollered back
10 decades later to Twitter followers/
Time travel on Steampunk cells
Home folks anxiously intercepting/
retweeting Instagram posts
When instead of checking for wi-fi/
their young men scanned for snipers

The ringtone of their generation:
a brass band playing
"When Johnny Comes Marching Home"
{hurrah/hurrah}
or the Colonel Bogey March
from the depths of dugouts
{set it on silent when they slip
over the top
lest a sniper hear & hone in on their
heart}
A full century after the Great War/
behind pale gravestones
ghosts on the former Western Front hold
spectral limbs out/

snap selfies in French & Belgian cemeteries after visiting hours
Post to retweet their Tweets
{with all the abbreviations & hashtags of the social media generation}
No email/no tinny voice messages on speaker or Bluetooth
Instead/in drawers & trunks amidst time-dulled medals
Those are their computer chips
loaded with data/old service records
We can read their posts/
encapsulating things that don't die:
The obscenity of war
The ferocity of a parent's love
The abomination that is
a child dying before his grandparent

Smell the TNT

Hear the whistle of the shell's arc
Feel the panic slip in the mud underfoot

#Hashtag that

TOP PHOTO by Daphne Vangheluwe: At the Menin
Gate, an observer records a portion of the Last Post
ceremony on her iPad. PHOTO LEFT, ABOVE: Soldier
mail from WWI, courtesy CanadianLetters.ca/VIU

EARLY TAKEN

Early in the war
Early promise broken hard
Forever sprawled at rest

PHOTO by Johan Declef: The Cimitiere de Laeken grave of Belgian soldier Max Pelgrims, who was 24 when he was killed on Aug. 19, 1914, not even three weeks after war was declared. Sculptor Ernest Salu's creation rests on Pelgrims' crypt in a private cemetery in Belgium. Pelgrims was the son of Eugene & Leonie Dailly.

LE CUPBOARD DE RESISTANCE

What's in my cupboard is my business
& if you wish to claim my house
for billeting your German officers
& move a good French woman
to the adjoining cottage of her own home,
you can carry my
very old cupboard for me, savez?

Let's hear it for Madame Belmont-Gobert
& her daughter Angele Lesur
They took a giant chance when Trooper Patrick Fowler
of the 11th Hussars/Prince Albert's Own
was cut off from his regiment 26 Aug 1914
in the Battle of Le Cateau
in German-occupied France
At risk of imprisonment/Mme. Belmont-Gobert hid
the Dublin native in a cupboard
that was 66 inches tall & 20 inches deep
She & her daughter kept Fowler safe
all four years of the war [3]

---

[3] The stakes were high for the French who sheltered escapees. One woman who sheltered a Commonwealth officer after Le Cateau was reportedly imprisoned, the escapee shot. When German soldiers occupied Mme. Belmont-Gobert's home, Fowler spent much of that time in her cupboard during the day, finally near war's end escaping to a neighbouring cottage disguised as an elderly woman. There he waited out the war. Mme. Belmont-Gobert's cupboard is on display at HorsePower, The Museum of The King's Royal Hussars at Winchester, UK. The War Office paid three years of Fowler's boarding allowance of 1.50 francs a day retroactively. Funds were raised for Mme. Belmont-Gobert when she faced poverty. She & Angele were in a Bertry-area resistance group presented to the King & Queen at Windsor Castle, & she was appointed an Honorary Officer of the Order of the British Empire, and her daughter an Honorary Member OBE. PHOTO: /Pixabay

SHADES OF WAR TO COME

1914 Christmas greeting card from Lt Col John Jenkins Penhale, an English engineer who settled in Sherbrooke, Que., leading the Divisional Ammunition Column of the CEF until his 1919 demobilization.

Courtesy CanadianLetters.ca

Majors
S. B. Anderson, C.F.A., Moncton, N.B.
G. H. Ralston, C.F.A., Port Hope, Ont.
J. T. McGowan, C.G.A. St. John N.B.

Captains
F. H. Greenlees, C.F.A., London, Ont.
Kenneth E. Kennedy, C.F.A., Sherbrooke, Quebec.
Percival T. Steen, C.G.A., Victoria B.C.

Lieutenants
C. Earl Churchill, C.F.A., Hantsport, N.S.
Hugh M. Dunlop, C.F.A., Hamilton, Ont.
R. St. C. Hayes, C.G.A., St. John, N.B.
J. B. Hoodless, C.F.A., Hamilton, Ont.
W. B. McTaggart, C.F.A., Clinton, Ont.
R. H. Moir, Ottawa, Ont.
H. S. Parker, C.F.A., Ottawa, Ont.
G. E. Magann, Toronto.
C. H. B. Garland, Ottawa.
F. A. Crathern, C.F.A., Montreal.
R. H. Harcourt, Welland, Ont.
R. P. Lefroy, Edmonton, Alberta.

Attached Officers
Lt.-Col. W. C. Good, C.F.A., Woodstock, N.B.
Captain H. Cook, C.F.A., Levis, Que.
Lieut. W. F. Smith, C.F.A., Kingston, Ont.

Warrant Officer
J. Slade, R.S.M., Kingston, Ont.

Christmas Greetings
and
Best Wishes for the New Year.
from
Lieut. Col. J. J. Penhale
and Officers

Divisional Ammunition Column,
First Canadian Expeditionary Force,
Salisbury Plain.

Xmas 1914.

#1915

16 Feb 1915:
First Canadian Division arrives in France
10 March 1915:
Battle of Neuve Chapelle
14-15 March 1915:
St. Eloi
22-28 April 1915:
Second Battle of Ypres. 6,000 Canadian casualties.
Germans use gas at Kitcheners Wood, Gravenstafel,
St. Julien, Frezenberg, Bellewaerde Ridge.
May 1915:
Second Battle of Artois: Aubers, Festubery, Givenchy
7 May 1915:
German U-boat sinks the luxury ocean passenger liner Lusitania
Sep – Oct 1915:
Third Battle of Artois: Loos, Bois Grenier, Hohenzollern Redoubt
17 Sep 1915:
Second Canadian Division arrives in France
Mar – Apr 1916:
St Eloi Craters
Italy declares war
on Austria & Germany in 1915.
Other Canadian WWI Theatres include:
Macedonia 1915-1917, Dardanelles 1915-1916, Egypt & Palestine 1915-1916

LIJSSENTHOEK

"We are the dead: short days ago, we lived, felt dawn, saw sunset glow." - John McCrae

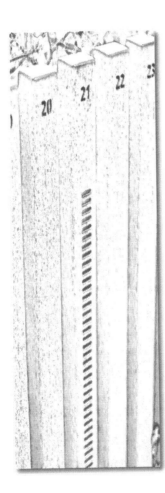

Publisher's
Clearinghouse
in reverse
Knock
at the door
at Remi
Quaghebeur
The widow with her
large brood
"We need
your farm
for a hospital
Just the right
place/close
to the front/
out of range
of shells/
Lucky you"
Imagine
her delight
Up come
carrots &
turnips
We plant

surgeons/
4,000 beds
We sow
bodies
Notches on iron
pickets mark
the number
of dead
each day/
a gruesome
calendar
Here only 35
of the
10,786
burials are
unidentified
with
the bones
that lie
beneath them
Lijssenthoek
is where
names match
bones

PHOTO by J. Carmichael photo/photo illustration Brad K. Larson
Metal fence pickets mark the days for the lifetime of the hospital at Lijssenthoek, Belgium — with notches noting how many were buried each day as the wounded continued to flow in from advanced dressing stations and clearing stations

HEADLINE: GREAT RESPECT TO BRAVE INDIAN HERO

Lt. Albert Mountain Horse
of the Blood Reserve:
The first Alberta First Nations man "allowed" to enlist
{Many First Nations are initially turned away from enlistment, only to be
subject to the draft in 1917 after conscription becomes law}
Lt. Mountain Horse is among
the very first Canadians to get to the battlefields of the
Western Front, landing in the Second Battle of Ypres

The Germans are shelling us now

He is among the first Allied soldiers to be gassed as German
forces unleash chlorine gas weaponized on the Western Front
on April 22, 1915 at St Julien/
After being gassed three times, consumption sets in
Invalided, Lt. Mountain Horse dies on his homeward journey
in military hospital in Quebec

My horse is wounded already

The *Macleod Spectator* of 2 Dec. 1915 records
older band members perform a war chant
as they join the funeral procession
Despite a heavy snowfall, the church is at overflow capacity
with an outpouring of grief, with both First Nations and settlers
in attendance together/unusual for the time, the paper notes
Town merchants close their stores, send wreaths in respect

The shells are whistling over our heads

Archdeacon Tims addresses the First Nations
at the funeral in their language,
reportedly a first for the pulpit in Macleod
The paper says it was the first known time
in the history of this church that burial service

is conducted over a First Nations person
His former schoolmaster, Rev. Sam Middleton
of the St. Paul school, is said to be broken up with loss
Lt. Albert Mountain Horse "cast a brilliant reflection
on the Blood Indians of Alberta," he says,
calling him "one of the Empire's greatest sons"

I have been up to the trenches for a long time now

The paper notes First Nations Chiefs attending
his funeral include Shot Both Sides, Weasel Fat,
Running Wolf, One Spot & Running Antelope
His comrade in arms, Lethbridge's Harry Watson,
is in attendance, missing a leg from war wounds
The last time he saw Mountain Horse was on the battlefield
Lt. Mountain Horse's father & three brothers
are among his pallbearers
On his coffin, his heartbroken mother
places her traditional headdress,
along with some of his belongings

The doctor said he was going to send me to the hospital.

I told him I would sooner die like a man

in the trenches than have a grave dug for me[4]

---

[4] Lt. Albert Mountain Horse is buried at the Old St. Paul Cemetery on the Blood Reserve. His words are bolded here. Mike Mountain Horse Elementary School in Lethbridge is named for Albert's brother, who joins up with brother Joe after Albert dies; Joe is wounded three times, & Mike gets buried alive by a shell at Cambrai, surviving Passchendaele. Both Mike & Joe return to Canada.

THE FINEST ACT OF THE WAR

Marshall Foch in 1919 called it that
On April 22/St Julien's Day/
toast the valour of
the Calgary Highlanders
with Highland Honours/
Glass held high to:
"The Glorious Memory of the 22nd of April 1915!"
Green horseman/new apocalypse:
fresh hells — a chemical terror emerges at Kitchener's Wood/
Evil green genii from tank of chlorine slinks across No Man's Land uncoiling at the enemy's
bidding/wafting on the breeze/Sinking in trenches/killing/
Shocking even Germans unleashing it/Horrified/wary/
they hang back/reluctant to advance through fumes/
failing to fully seize the moment
Stench of chlorine fills nostrils/sharp in throat & eyes/beyond bearing
Desperate for something white to wave/surrender
Genuine suffocation & pain behind the sternum
Each fast breath a small bomb, each cough the Grand Canyon
Retching in repentance of war/Tongue furry
Has he eaten a live wolverine? Inhaled a wasp hive?
Veins are rivers he will drown in/
Vertigo world bending buckling
Sure he's dying now/but at the ground he'd be dead {The air is certainly that fatal}
Who thought of this?/He can't speak for love but all's not fair in war
His friend will not wake/like others here/gone
Faces green-yellow/Cold blue gasp/sicked up blood-streaked/
Lapsing into sleep as bronchitis steals in/
fever rattles the brain into delirium
He wants   his mother[5]

---

[5] PHOTO: Behind the Barrage, from "Private Peat" by Harold Peat. The Fightin' 10th Canadian Battalion & the 16th Canadian Scottish Battalion were decimated in nightmarish nighttime counter-attack in the 2nd Battle of Ypres at Kitchener's Wood 22 April 1915 after being ordered to seal the French line broken following the first-ever chlorine gas attack. 75% losses devastated the troops. Forging on despite bad odds/ill planning in the first offensive operation by the Canadian Corps on Belgian soil, they were later awarded unique acorn/oak leaf titles worn on the shoulder. Canadian physician Dr. Francis A.C. Scrimger said soldiers should wet or urinate on their hankies for make-shift gas masks.

VANCOUVER CORNER

The weight of the war on stone shoulders
The brooding soldier at Vancouver
Corner/Saint-Julien/Langemark, Belgium
Wonder what he's thinking about
Looks like he's texting someone
Is he hashtagging
the First Canadian Division's
first engagement? #terribleNewWeapon
{168 tons of chlorine gas}
unleashed by the enemy nearby
on 22 April 1915?
Anger simmering
Veiled in Art Deco rock shadow
Is he thinking *Sandy Clark*
was killed today/
sniper shot him in the head/
Other things you can't #unsee?/
After {if/when} generations have forgotten,
he'll brood   still
Across the street at Vancouver Corner
a plaque recalls
Kamloops engineer Lt. Edward Donald
Bellew/machine-gun officer
With his troops destroyed & with the enemy less
than 100 yards away/
with no hope of reinforcements/he duked it out until the ammo failed
Then he seized a rifle/smashed the machine gun so the enemy couldn't use it/
and fought to the last before being taken prisoner 24 April 1915/
In 1919 after release from a POW camp/
Bellew discovered he was the first Canadian
awarded the Victoria Cross[6]

---

[6] PHOTO by J. Carmichael /PHOTO ILLUSTRATION Brad K. Larson:
WWI veteran Frederick Chapman Clemesha's "The Brooding Soldier" stands on Canadian soil with Canadian shrubs on officially Canadian territory, chiseled in a 10.5 metre shaft of granite where 18,000 Canadians withstood the first German gas attacks. Clemesha typed on his application: "For our part we do not wish to brag or glorify militarism. To a citizen soldier and to the parents of the 50,000 who did not return the thought of achievement and victory cannot be disassociated from the thought of sacrifice." Eventually troops were issued gas masks, and the Allied side used gas on the Germans. By Armistice 100,000 tons of it killed 40,000 troops.

IN {HIS} FLANDERS FIELDS

Put down the scalpel/pick up the pencil/
write the most famous war poem ever
In Flanders fields the poppies blow/Between the crosses, row on row
Not about choices you face as a doctor on the Western Front
We can save this one/We can help that one/
We can ease the pain for these ones
We can send home the effects of those ones/
We can't do anything for this one
We can't stop the flow of men/of bodies/of war
Days upon months/seasons upon years/
row on row of crosses
That mark our place: and in the sky/The larks still bravely singing fly
Scarce heard amid the guns below
You put down the scalpel & pick up the pencil/write the most famous war poem ever/
The words flow from that from flowers/poppies/riots/of scarlet/
unstaunched undeterred by explosions/unfailing in their return
Exhausted from battlefield medical practice/
from tending the victims of the 22 Apr 1915 gas attacks at nearby Kitcheners Wood
Bone weary 3 May 1915/
triaging in the advanced dressing station near the front
another ambulance/another casualty/
You, Lt. Col. Dr. John McCrae, will think
of Lt. Alexis Helmer/friend & former student lost at the Second Battle of Ypres
We are the dead: Short days ago,/We lived, felt dawn, saw sunset glow
Loved and were loved: and now we lie In Flanders fields!
Pilgrims bent on a quest to know of the war of their forebears seek you out
in the ghostly remains of the advanced dressing station
in an Essex Farm bunker in Belgium where you doctored
Makeshift clinic & morgue a stone's throw from the German trench
Ceiling sunk under the weight of a century's wars &
fragmented pieces of peace & poppies/
Your request then:
Take up our quarrel with the foe/To you, from failing hands, we throw
The torch: be yours to hold it high
Your torch flies through the air today/a dove/an olive branch/a hymn
*If ye break faith with us who die/We shall not sleep, though poppies grow/In Flanders fields**
We will keep faith with you if we can

_____

*Highlighted text by Lt. Col. Dr. John McCrae, from his poem "In Flanders Fields"

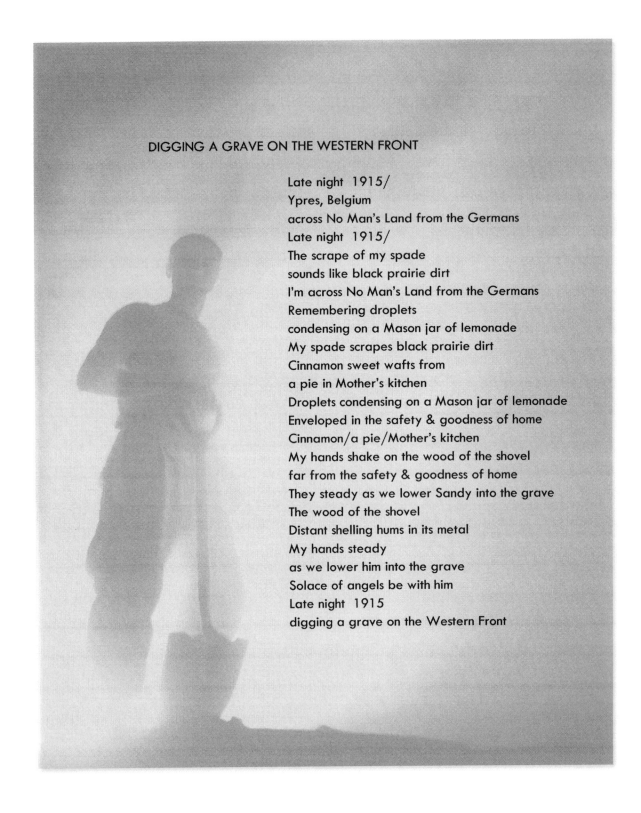

DIGGING A GRAVE ON THE WESTERN FRONT

Late night 1915/
Ypres, Belgium
across No Man's Land from the Germans
Late night 1915/
The scrape of my spade
sounds like black prairie dirt
I'm across No Man's Land from the Germans
Remembering droplets
condensing on a Mason jar of lemonade
My spade scrapes black prairie dirt
Cinnamon sweet wafts from
a pie in Mother's kitchen
Droplets condensing on a Mason jar of lemonade
Enveloped in the safety & goodness of home
Cinnamon/a pie/Mother's kitchen
My hands shake on the wood of the shovel
far from the safety & goodness of home
They steady as we lower Sandy into the grave
The wood of the shovel
Distant shelling hums in its metal
My hands steady
as we lower him into the grave
Solace of angels be with him
Late night 1915
digging a grave on the Western Front

ALL ABOUT YPRES/IEPER/WIPERS

Gothic beauty you/fair & ancient
Cloth Hall of leper spires/inspiring
The Grote Markt {great market}
In 1304 the world's textile capital/
guilds pitched your laces & damasks
You my lovely raging beauty/
The Great War's ground zero of
the key Ypres Salient /Your populace
evacuated away to safer territory
The bewitching worst stone in
the shoe of the German Imperial Army
They reduced you to rubble
in three extended pitched battles
but the Germans never held you

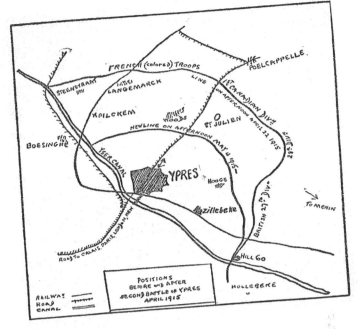

Halles d'YPRES.   La Salle Delbeke avant et après le Bombardement.
The Delbeke Hall before the Bombardment and after.
Visé Paris Nº 171014-117   Photo ANTONY Ypres

Affectionately the boys at the front
called you Wipers {can't imagine Y}
Half a million died trying to control you
Of the 66,000 Canadians
who died in the Great War/
1 in 4 died defending you
A portrait of you clad in the tatters of destruction
adorns the Canadian Senate Chamber
Restored stone by stone with reparations/
but who will restore our hearts & our brains?
Your destruction ~~wiped clean~~ but ours lingers long
Rechristened for sensible pronunciation
#leper exquisite & cobbled
A town-sized Old World museum you're exquisite/
like a snowglobe with a war-torn past
You steep visitors in the sepia tea of history/
where shells once brought medieval architecture
to her stone knees
The Last Post ceremony glowing at your heart/
the Menin Gate/
We too are shattered/in need of reparations for
years stolen/We are Ypres

PHOTOS: Left, Ypres postcard courtesy canadianletters.ca
top right, map from "PRIVATE PEAT" by Harold Peat

BLACK JACK/IN THE CORNER OF THE DUGOUT

I reckon I'll get dry eventually/
I hunker trying to look small
whilst all around me the shells they are a-flyin' & they're strafing again
   so if my spelling's bad don't blame me/blame Fritz
I'm doubled up in the corner of the dugout
under a hunk of tin trying to be itty-bitty as possible
The beggars don't care where they throw the darned shells
They are liable to hurt someone yet
Why, just the other day they broke up a perfectly good poker game/
Shell went off in our midst & injured three of us
I am supposed to be an artist at swearing
but I choke up whenever I start in on the devils
Last week we marched 42 km in a day
{a record by the way for the Canadian Corps}
rain every step
Fighting six days at Ypres/
four days with nothing to eat/
some boys never got any sleep
So much for armies marching on their stomachs
Sitting on sugar boxes to keep out of the water/
a coke brazier under my feet
If I turn every so often like a chicken on a spit/
reckon I'll get dry eventually

Postcard of British soldiers occupying former German dugouts CanadianLetters.ca / VIU

SAPPER DOROTHY LAWRENCE

An orphan with a dream
The original stunt journalist
Forbidden by French police
{"Non/Mademoiselle journaliste!"
In effect/they told you it takes balls}
You wondered what it would take for
a woman to get into the army
What it would be like
With the help of 10 'khaki accomplices'
A man's haircut/
razored face/
shoe polish tan
Tight corset doing no wonders
for a girlish figure
Cotton batting for shoulders
Lessons on drilling & marching
You passed as Pte. Denis Smith
/Leicestershire Regiment
for 10 days in the summer of 1915
{So/technically 'fake media'}
You were threatened
by the War Office
Ordered not to publish
Your eventual book is
an international hit /
but heavily censored/
would have been an Amazon bestseller
What a bold woman! Put THAT in your Kindle!
They can't take that away from you
Later you would be long institutionalized/
but not forgotten[7]

---

[7] Dorothy Lawrence's soldierly career as an undercover journalist was cut short when she got sick. She said she was threatened by the British War Office. After the war her book Sapper *Dorothy Lawrence: The Only English Woman Soldier* did well internationally but was heavily censored by the war office. She was eventually reported to have had some mental issues; she confided to a doctor that she was raped by her church guardian as a girl. She was deemed insane & committed to an asylum where she died decades later. She was buried in an unmarked pauper's grave. PHOTO: Wikipedia/public domain

Family photo courtesy Brian Vowel: Threshing on Vowel farm / Gibbon, Oklahoma
"Behind the Barrage" from "Private Peat" by Harold Peat (J. Carmichael photo illustration)

BLACK JACK/ANYWHERE BUT THERE

Wishing he was anywhere but there
A long way from Hays Kansas where he was born
To be still a kid there/sipping lemonade from a jelly glass
Walking beside the horses plodding in their traces with their soft clop-clops
Shelling purple-hulled peas on the porch in the Gibbon Oklahoma afternoon
in O-o-o-klahoma where everything is OK and the rumble you hear is surely
thunder in summer's silver-lined electric heat/not enemy shelling in the distance
On the other hand he'd have given something fine to be back in the Bullpound District
watching his brothers bust broncs at the rodeo/
asking a girl to two-step at a county dance/
or even sweating soot in the coal mine at the Crowsnest Pass
But there he is slogging it out/inch for inch at the point of the bayonet
Harvesting the enemy/They are pawns in a deadly stalemate/
all for Her, for sweet Ypres/If Ypres falls, Great Britain will go
Regal old cloth hall/now pretty much reduced to rubble
Skeletal/gaunt/darkened by shell blasts
Almost tired as they are
Wishing they were anywhere but   there

BLACK JACK/FED UP ON THE FRONT

*D*igging a kitchen behind the trench
Of all the concoctions that was ever cooked up/
we have them all skinned/
enough to give the devil indigestion
We take turns cooking fancy dishes
you will never see at any of the swell hotels
Yesterday we had Mulligan stew hobo-style
with whatever anyone could find
One of the boys made hard tack/bully beef
/oatmeal /dates/yes all together
We call it "Give & Take"
You take it because there's nothing else
/It gives you an ache

Set a spell/
a sign above the
door reads 'u r welcome
— a refuge for the sick, lame & lazy'
First here/first served is our motto
I brave brambles & snipers for blackberries for dessert
We'll have a bite mixed up for Fritzy
if he ever comes over -

- George 'Black Jack' Vowel

WHO WOULDN'T BE A SOLDIER?

"18 Aug 1915 ... We have tea & mud for breakfast/
skilly & mud for dinner/
& tea & mud for supper/Who wouldn't be a soldier?"

-Walter Thomas Robus, 1st Canadian Contingent bomb squad,
letter to Rev. Arthur Mansell Irwin, pastor of the Norwood
Methodist Church, of Norwood, Ontario

PHOTO: Top - Western Front life, from the photos of William John McLellan & Charley Groves & Dick Irwin enjoy ice cream in a photo studio (probably while on leave) — Herbert Laurier Irwin collection / Courtesy canadianletters.ca / VIU Above right - Christmas Dinner 1916, likely on leave, in Seaford England / From the collection of William John McLellan PHOTO: courtesy CanadianLetters.ca / VIU

NURSE EDITH CAVELL

Pioneer of modern
nursing methods
The British nurse
treated the wounded
of both sides
in German-occupied Belgium
helping 200
Commonwealth soldiers escape
Arrested/
she reportedly
said she did it
& that she wouldn't
stop
Death by
an executioner's bullet
for Nurse Edith Cavell
on 12 Oct 1915
sent shockwaves
around the world
sparking long debates
about the rules of war

Her words are inscribed near Trafalgar Square:
"Patriotism is not enough I must have no hatred
or bitterness towards anyone"[8]

8 Nurse Edith Cavell's death at the hands of the German firing squad was one of a number of reasons often cited for the US joining the First World War. The Church of England Calendar of Saints commemorates her on 12 October. In 1916, Mount Fitzhugh in Jasper National Park was renamed Mount Edith Cavell.

PHOTO/Public Domain: Nurse Edith Cavell with her dogs in her garden in peacetime Belgium. The dog on the right, Jack, was rescued after his mistress's death.

BLACK JACK/HOLIDAY TRUCE

S ay, talk about fireworks!
    On guard when New Year made her appearance
    The grandest display of fireworks ever let loose at once
      On the stroke of twelve,
5,000 rifles cracked
 flares by hundreds shot into the air:
Reckon that was the signal
The artillery opened up/ The country was lit for miles
After a couple minutes it died down quick as it started
We heard some fellows got to play
Christmas footy with Fritz last year
We were not so bold but
Gordie *stuck his head*
over the parapet
& wished Fritz a Happy New Year
Fritz's answer was typical:
a hail of bullets
I yells across No Man's Land
'Fritz, you got any resolutions?'
Fritz shouts asking if we have any
So I yells back in true spirit of
camaraderie "It isn't time for us yet
but when weather permits
we will make resolutions toward Berlin!"

     Fritz pulls triggers & makes unprintable remarks
     about British pigs
     As we're not British/
     we let it pass[9]

---

[9] So-called "holiday truces" were widely reported in 1914, with men from the two opposing sides briefly emerging from trenches into No Man's Land to exchange cigarettes, sweets & drink, show pictures of their sweethearts and families, and even play a game of football. "Fraternization" was quickly forbidden by those who wanted the war finished instead of stopped, but the trenches of both sides were so close together they could hear each other for exchanges such as the one George "Black Jack" Vowel described in excerpts from his letters to Louise "Bebe" Small Watson Peat here. Christmas card images (yes, cat memes even back then) from CanadianLetters.ca / VIU

62 BRITISH MACHINE GUNNERS WEARING GAS HELMETS.

#1916

2-13 June 1916
Battle of Mount Sorrel – 8,000 Canadian casualties

1 July 1916 – 18 Nov 1916
(1 July) Battle of The Somme opens.
Of 780 sent into Beaumont Hamel from Newfoundland Regiment, 684 killed or wounded
Battle of The Somme lasts until November 18, Canadians join in September
24,029 Canadian casualties. Somme battles include: Albert, Bazentin Ridge, Fromelles, High Wood, Pozieres, Guillemont, Ginchy, Flers-Courcelette, Thiepval Ridge, Le Transloy, Ancre Heights (capture of Regina Trench)

PHOTO: British machine gunners with gas masks/Postcard from CanadianLetters.ca

AMERICAN AVENGES LUSITANIA!

There are many tales buried here
Leland Wingate Fernald's headstone tells but one
New Hampshire man signed up with the Canadians
"A VOLUNTEER FROM THE U.S.A.
TO AVENGE THE LUSITANIA MURDER"
Handsome luxury ocean liner/so many mysteries
A torpedo from a German u-boat &
an unexplained inner explosion sank her off the Irish coast
For her & for them/he made it his war long before his
country did/dying a year & a day later
at Lijssenthoek hospital[10]

the boat is not forgot nor the will avenge her / the great war I am / nov. 11 1915 to enlist / bless her dead each one / Americans to enlist with the CEF/a painter from what Google streetview shows to be a modest neighbourhood 11 Nelson street /Dover N.J. /a driver with the 5th Brigade Canadian Field Artillery 2nd Canadian Division / I made it my war /only many decades later would the British government admit when a u-boat torpedoed Lusitania / she was carrying weapons / explosives / tools of war / at the time she was a recruiting propaganda tool of ocean liner proportions / a big part of the reason the U.S. entered the war in 1917 / ergo why I died of shrapnel wounds may 8 1916 / plot vi, row c / grave 36a

1,198 dead fallen into the chilly waters off the head of Kinsale 7 of May although my country is not yet ready to enter out of the u.s. army I cross to Esquimalt BC / protest the destruction of the Lusitania a century ago one of 40,000 / I die at lijssenthoek hospital

1915 / I Leland Wingate Fernald 476603 / God

---

[10] PHOTO by J. Carmichael: Gravestone / The sinking of the Lusitania was one of a number of reasons the US joined the war, although its status as a passenger liner has long been debated. Many Americans went before their country did. More than 35,000 soldiers in the CEF listed their birthplace as the U.S. or Alaska. When the U.S. entered in April 1917, they did so with decisive force and at great loss. In the remaining year-and-a-half of the war, from a country of 92 million, there were 116,708 American military deaths and almost twice as many wounded. Today, the National WWI Museum and Memorial in Kansas City ranks as a top American museum, and tells the stories of America in World War I.

" Excuse me ! Your standing in my shaving water."

BLACK JACK/sHELL-hole

Stumbling into a hell-hole/
rather a sHELL-hole
He sputters to the surface
Coming up through murk
for putrid air
Treading on sodden fabric & flesh
Air bubbles escaping into
the flailing open arms
"of dead Boches"
where the anguish
of the battle pools
Vacant blue eyes
& rubbery fingers
will haunt him for decades

PITCHED BATTLE

Fritzy's fighting like
a bloody double-distilled
son-of-a-seacook

PACKAGE HAIKU

Don't put anything
in that you can't eat /Other
things are useless

{A coded message/
You'd have to read between the lines
To understand he's starving}

(Excerpt/letter home from
David McLean of CanadianLetters.ca)

POSTCARD: Thomas Poolton collection /Courtesy canadianletters.ca / VIU

MORTS POUR LA FRANCE

PHOTOS, Steven Van Den Eynde: a Muslim memorial at Verdun {Fought from 21 Feb – 18 Dec 1916} is dedicated "Aux soldats Musulmans morts pour la France" – to the Muslim soldiers who died for France. The Battle of Verdun was the largest, most costly one between the Germans & the French. Casualty estimates (for both wounded & killed, both sides) approach a million.

A STOWAWAY'S SECOND GRAVE

Stowed away at 14
Determined to go to the Great War battlefields
What note did he leave his mother in 1915?
Too young/Too stubborn/ Don't go Freddie
We hardly knew ye
Forever a Halifax schoolboy
Felled as a sapling/dismantling his folks' dreams
First interred where he fell on May 11, 1916
A still-green leaf amongst the maples
"Their Glory Shall Not Be Blotted Out"
Says his grave stone/his first destroyed by shells
during the Battle of Mount Sorrel
One of 230 casualties whose second stone
at Maple Copse Cemetery also says
"known to be buried here" [11]

WORKING PARTY AT THE MAPLE COPSE DEBACLE/CHARLES HENRY SAVAGE

All work of this sort had to be done at night and under severe machine gun and shell fire, but even had this not been the case, Maple Copse still would have presented an almost impossible task. What had once been a thick woods was now a tumbled mass of blasted trees and upturned earth, and amongst this debris were the bodies of hundreds of Canadians and Germans. The ground had been fought over almost continuously for twelve days during hot and rainy weather, and the stench from it was sickening. A poor place to give men their first taste of war. Certainly it was no psychologist who ordered these working parties."
– Charles Henry Savage, Eastman, Quebec, enlisted in 1915 with the 5th Canadian Rifles

[11] PHOTO: J. Carmichael/ Pte. Frederick Freeman Laing from Halifax was buried at Maple Copse Commonwealth Cemetery. He was 14 when he stowed away on the SS Caledonian along with stowaways Dr. Leo Landry & Dr. Augustine McNulty, Dr. Joseph Molloy & E. Carroll (a.k.a. Naylor), Thomas O'Meara & A. Shaw. Laing was buried, but then his first grave was destroyed a month later, along with 229 others, as shells tore up the graveyard during the Battle of Mount Sorrel. Troops then had to go in "working parties" to re-inter the bodies, prompting the inscription "known to be buried here." Will Bird's memoir, "And We Go On" describes this process in piercing detail.

FOR NEWFOUNDLAND

So alone at Gallipoli
The only North American regiment in
the bloody fray
Nearly extinguished at
Beaumont-Hamel 1 July 1916
Your mothers
& grandmothers
& sweethearts
raise the cost of bronze tablets
to honour you across the sea
Your names/
seared on their hearts
A cost too great to be borne:
The abomination that is
a grandchild survived by
his grandmother

PHOTO by Andrew Mackay: the memorial caribou at Masnieres. The people and government of Newfoundland built five monuments in France & Belgium in the form of a caribou. These are at; Beaumont-Hamel, Gueudecourt, Monchy-Le-Preux, Courtrai and Masnieres. [12]

---

[12] At the time of the Great War, Newfoundland was not a Canadian province. Its contribution as a separate British dominion, was disproportionately large. Contributing 12,000 military personnel from a pre-war population of 242,000. Some 35 percent of men 19-35 served by 1918. More than 6,200 served with the Newfoundland Regiment. Near Beaumont Hamel, on the opening day of the Somme offensive, July 1, 1916, there were 710 killed, wounded or missing, out of 801 present in a 30-minute attack on German positions. Newfoundlanders also served forestry, naval, and military units. Famed for their sailing, Newfoundlanders filled the colony's naval reserve with 2,000 sailors & fishermen. Others served on allied military and merchant ships; of 500 known merchant sailors, 1 in 5 died.

After brutal casualty rates caused volunteer rates to plummet, compulsory service became law in April 1918 in Newfoundland, as it had in Canada in the fall of 1917. Support or the lack of it divided on largely religious and eco-political lines. July 1 is now Memorial Day in Newfoundland & Labrador.

The bronze caribou that stands at the Beaumont Hamel memorial is dedicated to the 1st Battalion of the Royal Newfoundland Regiment. Tablets bear the names of the 814 Newfoundlanders who died in service in the First World War but have no known graves. (WarMuseum.ca) The tablets were placed with the support of the women of Newfoundland, a lot of money raised to make sure the lads were properly acknowledged.

703472 PTE WILLIAM LOWRY 102 /CANADIAN (to his mother)

Trench warfare is so hideous that I will not
harrow you with any description of it /
I have been in action (on a machine gun)
at Ypres Salient (at Hill 60) and on the
Somme, where our battalion 'went over'
& took Regina Trench
What renders the fighting so appalling
is the artillery fire
On the Somme it is continuous / day &
night/world without end
The sacred historian of the Deluge wrote that
'the windows of Heaven were opened'
Had he been recording the battle of the Somme
he would have said that
the whole side wall
had come out!" [13]
- William Lowry

BLACK JACK/PUTTING UP A FIGHT

Fritz won't find Tommy
asleep/Boys throwing everything
but the wheels at him
PHOTO: Victory Bond poster by Arthur
Keelor/Ontario Government Archives

[13] William Lowry immigrated to British Columbia before the war, then enlisted. After being severely burned in a dugout, he was treated in France and England before being sent to Qualicum Military Convalescent Hospital at Qualicum Beach, B.C. in 1917. He wrote to his family of his convalescence: "I am now in pretty good health. The skin on my face and hands is now quite strong. I have been having massage treatment for the neck which has already relaxed nearly all the contraction of the skin there. The hair on the eyelids has been restored. The convalescent life at this place has completed that wonderful medical work which was begun in Rouen ... The place where I am now is situated about 110 miles from Victoria and about 30 miles from where our battalion trained. Formerly a seaside hotel, it is equipped with all facilities for golf, lawn tennis, bowling greens, boating and fishing which are indulged in by the returned men who are convalescing here, of whom there are about 120 ... Everything is very quiet here. The weather is sultry without much rain. The cedars and Douglas fir stands 300 ft high .... With best wishes to you all / I am your loving Willie."- /CanadianLetters.ca/VIU

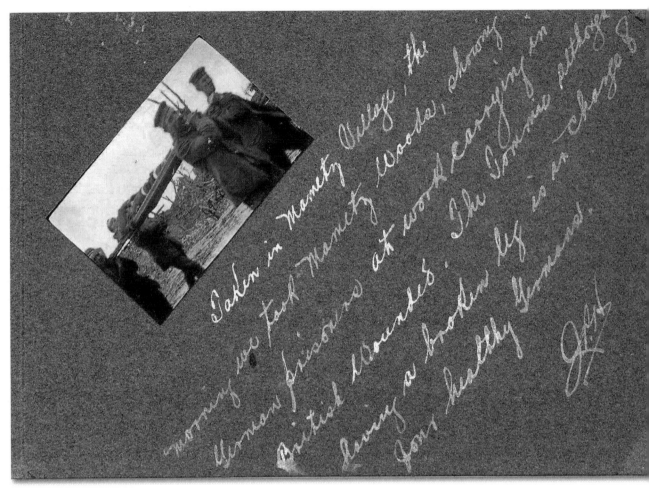

SCRAPBOOK HAIKU/WALTER JAMES LANTZ/25/ 92921/P.E.I.

He's not coming back from
The Somme/His chum sent this book
of pictures/We grieve

He's made this scrapbook
So you can see your son's life
Before he was cut down[14]

---

[14] Walter James Lantz enlisted at Charlottetown in October, 1915. A gunner with the 98th Battery / Cdn. Garrison Artillery, he was killed at The Somme 12 July 1916. A friend compiled a scrapbook for his parents. Lantz's gravestone at Becordel-Becourt, reads: "The Lord Thee Keeps." In the lower picture, the wounded British soldier on the stretcher is in charge of the "four healthy German" POWs carrying him. Photos / CanadianLetters.ca / VIU

OVER THE TOP/{SONG FOR GEORGE MORTON BIRD}

CHORUS:

A^m D^m E^7 A^m

Over the top / Over the top / Out of the trench & over the top

A^m D^m E^7 A^m

Got no clue if or when this war will ever stop/until then the boys & I go over the top

Over the top's the thing for an infantryman here
bombs, sandbags, shovel, trench flares, carry your own gear
My boots are wet but my helmet's set / don't worry my dear
250 rounds of ammo, a rifle & a lucky bottle of beer & we go (over the top)

Just a quarter of our lot made it "over the top" that day
Fighting went on for months/bloody casualties all the way
Worst ever in British history/The Somme was hell to pay
A million lads were dead by the battle's end they say 'Cause they went (over the top)

The prisoners they flinched with the spooky whistling sound
Their own German shells a-flying high/exploding all around
Artillery fire everywhere we're desperate for safe ground
The whole darn thing was smithereens before it all went down & we went (over the top)

All rights reserved / Jacqueline Carmichael {inspired by letters of George Morton Bird, Port Alberni BC, convalescing in Britain from wounds sustained at the Somme. Bird died of wounds sustained in the Battle of Arras 6 May 1917.} PHOTO: Ready to go over, from "Private Peat" by Harold Peat.

IN THE FIELD TO WIN

When he'd play rugby, she used to tell him to stay unhurt/to play "well back"
Margaret Walteria Milroy never fully believed her son was dead
She left a light on in his room/{in maternal denial/Who could blame her?}
hoping he'd come home/find his way up the path
Lt. Eric "Puss" McLeod Milroy of the Black Watch {an accountant with a master's degree
& an international rugby player}

wrote his mother:
"We are in some slight trouble
to-morrow/ So I am just warning you
there is to be no 'keeping well back'
then"

Five scant days later he was killed at
Delville Wood 18 July 1916 at The
Somme /honoured on the Thiepval
memorial to the missing dead
The light stayed on upstairs
Just in case

A Rugby Players Memorial was
dedicated in 2017 on the Chemin
des Dames Battlefields /"Rugby
Players Trench" where on 16 Sept
1917, 15 international troops who
played the game together perished
together[15]

PHOTO by Stephen Kerr, SK
Photography: Delville Wood today.

---

[15] John Dennison / ex-rugby player and official / organizes commemorative rugby tournaments & memorials. He and Franck Viltart from the Conseil Department L'Aisne launched World Rugby Memorial Project in October 2015 at the World Rugby Museum at Twickenham Stadium, with a monument designed by former French rugby captain Jean-Pierre Rives, was unveiled at Craonnelle in 2017. Of Eric Milroy, Dennison said: "A man who was a born leader, and always at the centre of the action, Milroy, like many rugby players of his time came through private education, and when enlisting was made an officer. There are many examples of these men who were killed in WWI, with them leading from the front."

BLACK JACK/MEDAL LEDGER FOLIOS RECEIPT

Before — June 1916
Break the Germans' Thiepval line at the Somme!
Mouquet Farm, Pozieres 10/11 Sept 1916
Private George Vowel/10th Batt/Lewis gun/Post 77
{right in the middle of this map, courtesy the UK government & Stephen Kerr}

After — October 1916
Demolished/pulverized beyond recognition/the UK government aerial photos show the road
gone/trenches gone/farm gone/{they don't show buddies gone, but they're gone}
He "kept his Lewis Gun working perfectly and was largely responsible for our continued possession of
this post"/There's a world of damage between those lines

The medal/ awarded a month later/ lasted/The promotion did not.
He was demoted for going AWOL & for getting into fisticuffs with an Australian soldier.
Black Jack wrote this cranky found haiku: *"Drills by Sam Hughes himself/Something seemed to be eating
him/Probably lousy!"*

PHOTO by Stephen Kerr

BLACK JACK/FETCH THE HORSES

My Maverick
My good cayuse
Not much to look at but he'd do
whatever I asked of him/Smart
Took me through a blizzard
to a Christmas dance
Got snowed in & stayed a week
Maverick stayed too
Cozy in a stall/plenty of hay
Good cutting horse
Spoiled that horse
Loved that horse

Mav carried his little brothers & sister to school three astride

innocent peacetime faces awreath in smiles

at the prospects of recess

& kind pretty Miss Lennie /

Some small bit of Mother's home-made bread & butter from the churn/

wrapped in their kerchiefs

Maverick would wait outside at the post patient for his bit of water & hay

the return trip over the dusty prairie road to modest barn with sod roof

The War Monster needed all the horses

that could be mustered

Equine pawns perished without medals

The French government came to the Canadian prairies to buy horses for $135 apiece

TOP PHOTO: Pack horses & mules transport ammunition to the 20th Battery, Canadian Field Artillery in Neuville St. Vaast, France/April 1917 PHOTO: public domain/postcard

PHOTO LEFT: courtesy Brian Vowel: Prairie horses being driven by cowboys. According to The Horse in War and Famous Canadian War Horses (David Sobey Tamblyn), 24,000 Canadian mounts survived past Armistice to Belgian government auction. At least 110 officers brought their chargers home to Canada.

THE WAR HORSE

Poppy grazes forever at Ascot/No fear of flying shrapnel
The high ominous whistle of shells but a distant/haunting echo in tall bronze ears
No more 3,000-pound guns to pull/No more charges to carry her master into
Articulated metal ribs on the War Horse Memorial
Designed by British sculptor Susan Leyland
Poppy reflects the deprivations of war
Her eternal hopes now to fatten up on good grass
Poppy has earned green pastures
& still waters & carrots
Both indispensable & disposable,
more horses than people/8 million horses & mules/
would die in the Great War
If you asked Poppy she might question
if there was anything "Great" about it
Who can bear the thought of horses dying in a war
in which they sought only to serve their masters/
or fathers & sons & sweethearts who met similar fates
as they sought only to serve their masters
Good horse/Poppy [16]

---

[16] TOP RIGHT PHOTO courtesy TheWarHorseMemorial.org. Above, the British War Medal, issued to many soldiers, including George "Black Jack" Vowel. (Photo courtesy Brian Vowel)

BALLARAT

"He paweth in the valley, and rejoiceth in his strength;
He goeth forth to meet the armed men. He mocketh at fear, and is not afraid,
Neither turneth he back from the sword."

PHOTO by Peter Kervarec: A bronze memorial at Ballarat, Australia honours horses and mules killed in World War I – and poet Adam Lindsay Gordon. Designed by Raymond B. Ewery. Base engraved with Job 39:21-22. The memorial was erected by The Adam Lindsay Gordon Society to mark the 100th anniversary of the poet's living in Ballarat. "Also as a memorial to the 958,600 horses and mules killed in The First World War, Including 196,000 that left these shores never to return." According to the Australian War Memorial site, one horse made it back to Australia – Sandy, the horse belonging to Maj. Gen. Sir William Bridges (who was killed at Gallipoli.) Sandy was sent from Gallipoli to Egypt to France and then to England, before being sent to live out his days at the Central Remount Depot at Maribyrnong, Australia.

In Canada, a horse named Morning Glory outlived her master, Lt.-Col. George Harold Baker, MP, by catching the eye of top brass. Safe for the war's duration, she returned to graze in Brome, Quebec after the hostilities. Like soldiers, horses that died during the sea journey to deployment were buried at sea.

"Of the 750 horses taken on board at St. John 7 of them were lost at sea thru sick-ness. Sharks followed us daily after the first horse had been thrown over-board. We were eleven days making the trip ... " – recorded Joseph Richard Boucher of Kent County, New Brunswick.

On 22 Nov 1914, at Salisbury Plain, England (training),James Wells Ross wrote: "Today we had no church parade owing to the cold weather so we took everyone out for a ride and it did the horses good ... The horses stand the weather well, but need lots of care and exercise often to keep them warm. I have a fine one now. 'Ben' I call him. He is dark bay almost black with a star and left ear split for about half an inch. He is full of life and never gets tired." /CanadianLetters.ca

AT ALL COSTS/AT BULLY-LES-MINES

Run with the message/the message of utmost importance
Take the message to the brigade at all costs
The regiments have been cut off/cut off endangering the battle's outcome
Reinforcements needed for the regiments
Corp. Fernand Marche
Galibot from age 13 in the Bethune/France pit mine
husband to Angelina Louisa Maria/father of two precious children
volunteer/emerge from a shell-hole
Run with your valour/run for your life
The battle is at risk/
at risk of being lost to the enemy
You volunteer to risk all in this perilous duty
Shell fire wounds you/Wounds you mortally 1 August 1916
But mortal wounds cannot quench your resolve/Corp. Fernand Marche
Crawl to the path/hoist the message wallet high
If you must die/as your life ebbs /lift the wallet high
As rigor mortis sets in/the liaison spies the wallet
The Front/& the battle's outcome/
secured by your valour/
secured even in your death

PHOTO by Geerhard Joos; PHOTO ILLUSTRATION/Brad K. Larson

1ST

Munitions worker
Lottie Meade

MUNITIONETTE/CANARY

Beautiful attitude/
Hand on her hip
Lottie Meade/
a mother of four
Self-confident
Proud to do her bit
for homefront service
The "Rosie the Riveter"
of her era
"Essential" work
with hazardous munitions
meant better wages/
the title "Munitionette"
Long hours & six-day weeks
making explosives
meant more risk
Munitions plants
had improper ventilation
Poor working conditions
Toxic chemicals meant
yellowed skin
& the nickname "Canaries"
For Lottie/TNT poisoning
A UK Royal Mail stamp in 2016
remembers Lottie Meade

Lottie Meade Stamp /

U.K. Royal Mail

RECRUITING ADS HAIKU
Free Men To Fight!
Great opportunities
for a great war!

CLICKETY-CLICK
50 Skilled Female
Stenos / Army QC Corps!
Adventure In France!

BONJOUR!
Phone Operators
For Army Switchboards Near Front
Parle French SVP!

FILET IT/FIX IT/FILE IT OR FIGURE SOMETHING
ELSE OUT!
Queen Mary's Army
Auxiliary Corps In France
Cook/Fix/File Or Misc!

FARM SERVICE CORPS!
Just-For-Now Help Out!
Women Replace Men Gone To Front!
Appropriate Work!

GOOD JOB TIL ARMISTICE!
13k Women
Stateside Active US Navy
While Men Are Away!

NURSE – SEE THE WORLD!
Your Nation Needs You!
France/Belgium/Homefront CEF!
Adventure! Duty!

*"All our troops are very optimistic these days. We have the
Huns on the run all over. We all expect to be home soon."*
Eugene Robert Drader, 25, to his parents
12 Sept 1916 / four days before his death

DEAR MR. & MRS. DRADER,

This is without doubt the hardest task I have ever had to do -
telling you of the death of your son and my best friend ...

Two days before we went into action I had transferred to 'D'
Company to be with Eugene, little thinking that our long and
intimate friendship was to end so suddenly and so tragically....
He was buried near where he fell - a real soldier's burial, not
the parade style of military funeral, but the short hesitating
prayer that was said over his grave, with our heads bowed
very low on account of machine gun fire, the most sincere
prayer ever offered up ...

He was the best friend I ever had ... Since his death I am not the same; I cannot be; but everyone is
kind & I have received much kind sympathy, for we were known as inseparables ... As deeply as I feel
it, it can be nothing in comparison with your feelings .

... I wish you knew the excellent influence he has had on the lives of the young who knew him as their
teacher. They worship him, and what is more, they try to imitate him. Many, many hearts in Edmonton
and Gull Lake will be very, very sad...

It seemed at first that no one could be more heartbroken than I myself; and I took chances for over a
day in the front line that I never would have taken otherwise; I seemed to be obsessed with the one
idea, that Eugene and I must not be separated.

But I know there's nothing to compare with father's and mother's love, so I send you sympathy and I
mean it more than I ever meant those words before ... I share your sorrow, words cannot say how
deeply.

Yours with sincerest sympathy,
         Harry E. Balfour, Lieut. 49th Bn. Canadians" [17]

---

[17] Eugene Robert Drader was born in London, Ontario. A teacher in Edmonton, he was killed in action while with
the 49th Battalion on 16 Sept. 1916. Excerpts from letter/images Courtesy Canadianletters.ca / VIU; Photo
illustration Brad K. Larson

1 OCT 1916/TO-DAY I AM AT "DIVISIONAL REST CAMP, WARBOY"

The Germans tried repeatedly to get our dugout with a shell where we had some stretcher cases /At last, Fritzie got a direct hit on the roof/Owing to it being an extra heavily timbered roof/the shell did not burst inside But it bashed the roof in and drove a beamdown on my head, forced my front teeth out a bit and splintered all the front ones

After I had recovered myself, I ran out to a near-by dug out with three comrades, all of us dazed ... we went back and helped get the stretcher cases back 1.5 miles to our batt'n doctor's dug-out at the bottom of a shell hole and then 30 feet under the ground / While sitting there in the dug out, trying to eat something, tho' I had no appetite, I collapsed and cried like a baby

I want to stay and help our brave stretcher-bearers out with the rest of the gallant fellows who were lying out in the front line, wounded, but a day, a night, and a day with nothing to eat, fighting or working continuously, with no sleep/and at last/ this crack on the head did me...

So I went out with three other walking cases
We managed to walk overland, dodging German whiz-bangs all the time/
to the advanced dressing station 5 miles farther back ...

Out of the 4 battalions of the 4th Brigade of 3,000 men, there is not over 250 left/

A smiling Canadian

Of our battalion about 35 are left
But even yet I heard that all that were left were ordered to charge forward again

From the diary of George Hedley Kempling, enlisted in Toronto/returned after the war, CanadianLetters.ca / VIU
ENVELOPE PHOTO TOP RIGHT: CanadianLetters.ca / VIU
PHOTO LEFT: A smiling Canadian, from "Private Peat" by Harold Peat

BLACK JACK/NASTY RUMOUR

Somebody spread a rumour {Somebody happy to be home}
Somebody said they saw me at the front/
hunkered over German dead
cutting crosses into their chests with my Bowie knife
Tickled my brother but not Mother
Somebody who was missed by the Canadian boys
still manning the trenches
They were still fodder/
still there & it was still hell
There was enough unsubstantiated recruitment propaganda
about Fritz committing atrocities
without some joker spreading tales back home
that Black Jack had joined those "revenging"
the {unsubstantiated legend of} the rumoured 'crucified soldier'
A Canadian alleged to have been found nailed to a cross with Fritz's bayonets
Nobody saw it/many claimed to know somebody unnamed who saw it
His Mother would weep/letting out her hairpins
brushing her thin long hair at night before bed
in tears at the idea of a damaged boy/
feral from war/gouging the bodies of the slain
I'll live to drag a dead cat across somebody's grave yet
When he got home {if he got home} *Somebody will hear from me*
Maybe just to scare him he could bring his   Bowie knife

PHOTO: Soldier life/courtesy CanadianLetters.ca / VIU

MILUNKA SAVIC/THE ORIGINAL HUNGER GAMES

They say some are meant
to be soldiers/some aren't
Well/Milunka agreed
so she pretended to be her brother

When the Serb army called him up
she went in his place/
the original Hunger Games
in disguise
Alas/her gender was uncovered
when she was wounded

She asked to return to the field
her commanding officer said he'd
answer her "tomorrow"
"I'll wait," she said

Not budging/ just waiting
Embodying guts & chill
After an hour of
her standing there
{how unnerving was that}
he grudgingly agreed
she could stay in the army
Good thing too

The odds were "ever in her favour"
She's the top-honoured
female fighter
Ever [18]

---

[18] Milunka Savic went on to become the most decorated female fighter in the history of warfare, period. In 1916, she captured 23 Bulgarian soldiers - by herself. Hers are the French Légion d'Honneur (twice)/the Cross of St. George/the Most Distinguished Order of St Michael (English) & the Serbian Miloš Obilić Medal. She was also the only female recipient of the Croix de Guerre (French) with the palm attribute. To top it off, in World War II, she courageously refused to attend a prestigious dinner with occupying Nazis. For that she earned 10 months in jail. After a brief marriage and having a child, she went on two adopt two orphans. She lived a long life, dying at 81. There's a street in Belgrade named for her. (Photo public domain/courtesy Wikipedia)

BLACK JACK/THEM OR HIM

An address: Paul Dilschmann
of Weissenfels Germany
Words he can't make out
in a language he doesn't know
Clean slate white pages/grey grid lines
The kind of pocket notebook
you pick up at any stationers
or find on a body emptied of its stories
by a Lewis gun
He is miles from a stationers store
Its former scribe lies on the shell-scarred field
He crosses out addresses that don't pertain to him
when he commandeers the book bought in Germany
& tucked into a German uniform pocket
He makes notations anyone/Canadian or German/might make:
Walked four miles for a bath today/
Sandy died from a sniper's bullet yesterday
How strange our company's brass band sounds
in a big French wood
Sunday morning at the front
Trying to make myself small in the corner
against a hail of shrapnel

He fills between covers with desperate scrawlings
He may think of the Dilschmann family/
   They won't see this journal because
      He plucked it from that mud/
      lifted it from that body
   on the Western Front 11 Oct 1916/
but not the day he earned
   the Military Medal for bravery/
      apparently for single-handedly
         taking out a bunch of Germans at the Somme/
         when it was either them or him that had to go

An address: Paul Dilschmann of Weissenfels Germany
Words he can't make out in a language he doesn't know

PHOTO by J. Carmichael: Journal of Paul Dilschmann & George "Black Jack" Vowel

Sgt. Maj. FLORA SANDES

A British woman who liked to drive/
adventure/ rebel
Nursing was the way to be part of the war
as men got to do
She formed the Women's Sick & Wounded
Convoy through a fortuitous mix-up while
working for St John Ambulance in Serbia
& for safety — & to get food rations —
she enrolled in the Serbian army
quickly rising through the ranks
to Sergeant Major
Wounded by a grenade in hand-to-hand
combat in 1916, she earned the highest
decoration of the Serb military
— the Karadorde Star
Also in 1916/she wrote a memoir/
An English Woman-Sergeant in the Serbian Army
After her injury, she ran a hospital and raised funds for the Serbian Army
After demobilization in 1922 she lectured extensively around the world
& published a second memoir
She returned to England after being interned {with her husband} by the Nazis in 1941
In 2009 a street in Belgrade was named for her
Here she is on a kick-@$$ Serbian stamp/
one of a series of six honouring British women
for humanitarian work in WWI/
designed by Marina Kalezić
Go Flora

Serbian stamp honouring Sandes

BATTLE HAIKU for Sgt. Maj. FLORA SANDES

Some might rather fill
their shoes at the Western Front
than sit & weep here

AN IMAGINED LETTER TO THE TRUE MRS. AMY BEECHEY

"Dear Mrs. Beechey
The King & I wish to thank you for
your splendid sacrifice {to the War Monster}.
Five of your eight sons died for the Glorious Cause
Five crosses hewn in their honour from the Lincoln Cathedral stone
have been strewn around the world

One for Lance Cpl. Harold/26/a farmer & ANZAC/who survived Gallipoli only to die
of a whiz-bang on the Western Front

One for Pte. Charles/39/a teacher & naturalist
who died from wounds in the chest
at Dar es Salaam in Tanzania

One for 2nd Lt. Frank/30/ a teacher & cricketer/
who died repairing communications cables
between trenches in France

One for Sgt. Barnard/38/a mathematician & teacher killed in
action at the Battle of Loos

One for Rifleman Leonard/a railway clerk/with the London Irish
Rifles / Dead from wounds in an enemy gas attack near Rouen,
France
His last words/according to TheLincolnshireRegiment.org/were
'My darling mother/don't feel like doing much yet.
Lots of love, Len.'

Thank you, Mrs. Beechey, their beloved mother/
for your sacrifice!"
Signed/Queen Mary

"Dear Queen Mary/Your Majesty:
It was no sacrifice/Ma'am. I did not given them willingly."
Signed/Mrs. Amy Beechey [19]

---

[19] PHOTO: Geerhard Joos /grave of 2nd Lt. Frank Beechey. This letter is imagined, but Mrs. Amy Beechey
actually said those words to Queen Mary when she met her in person / after Queen Mary thanked her for her
sacrifice

LIFE LESSONS OF A WORLD WAR I SOLDIER

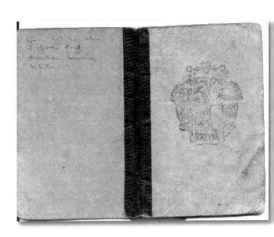

While there are terrible things to be learned on the
battlefield/
things that will have to be studiously unlearnt later/
there are some chestnuts to be gathered/tucked in a journal
in war, that school of the hardest of all possible knocks, such as:
Take care of your feet/Keep your kit dry/Learn how to
mend/Don't be lippy/Mind your step/Keep your head
down/Laugh when you can/Make a will
Sometimes it's best to stay put/sometimes it's best to get out of
there fast/wise the soldier who knows the difference
In lieu of an umbrella/or a roof/a rubber sheet will do in a pinch
The hungrier you get/the more willing you are to eat weird combinations of things
A lot of things will do/in a pinch/It could always be worse/you don't want to know how/
and sometimes it is
Making lists for the future can help keep sanity in a tough spot
A hot bath is one of life's greatest gifts
Sometimes you really need something to eat/Everyone could use a little R&R now & then
Communications with the home front are a lifeline/Things look different when you're desperate
Enjoy nature/even if it's just a fallen leaf: you will feel a tiny bit better
If you can't do anything about miles of mud/do what you can to make it cozy
Know how to make yourself comfortable as possible in a tough spot
Have a happy thought that can comfort you
Don't be too surprised if the lines that were drawn last year are different this year
If you think you're depressed, you may just be in a war zone
There are few things that can't be lost/war is not one of them
Some battles take so much to win it's a net loss
You don't fight for King or Kaiser/
You fight for the guy next to you in the trench & you think of your family while you're about it
Prepare yourself for when things get better
There will be things you don't have time or energy to think about now
Tough times don't last/tough people do (unless your number's up, then that's it)
Sometimes you just have to put one foot in front of the other & keep going
You'll feel better about yourself if you can spare someone else a little dignity
Be there for the person standing beside you in the trench
Be nice if you can, everyone has their own lot to manage/Learn to nap anywhere
Don't take propaganda hook/line & sinker
Like war, life is like milking a cow:
If you're lucky, you get up tomorrow & you get to do it all over again

PHOTO: Journal from CanadianLetters.ca

#1917

January 1917:
Not-so-secret secret Zimmermann Telegram from German Foreign Office proposes military alliance between Germany & Mexico: if the U.S. enters the Great War against Germany, Mexico to Texas, Arizona & New Mexico; infuriates U.S. officials

Prisoners going to the rear

February 1917:
Germany goes all-out in submarine warfare to control the North Atlantic

6 Apr 1917:
U.S. Congress votes to declare war on Germany

Apr-Jun 1917:
Battle of Arras – Vimy Ridge, First Scarpe, Second Scarpe, La Coulotte, Arleux, Third Scarpe, Affairs south of the Souchez River, Avion

9 to 12 Apr. 1917:
Battle of Vimy Ridge. Canadians use "creeping barrage" to storm and seize the ridge, with British and French help. 10,602 Canadian casualties

Jun-Dec 1917:
Third Battle of Ypres – Messines, Pilckem Ridge, Langemark, Menin Road Ridge, Polygon Wood, Broodseinde, Poelcappelle, 1st & 2nd Passchendaele, Cambrai

15-25 Aug 1917:
Battle of Hill 70

29 Aug 1917:
Conscription passes in Canada

26 Oct to 14 Nov 1917:
Canadian Corps at Battle of Passchendaele.

6 Dec. 1917:
Devastation as the Halifax Explosion kills 1,630: munitions ship collides with another vessel in harbour , sends Canada's civilian war dead numbers skyrocketing

Dec. 1917:
Americans declare war on Austria

17 Dec. 1917:
Canadian federal election polarized by conscription

By 1917:
Every continent, all oceans are in the war (The US came in in April 1917)

PHOTO RIGHT: Prisoners going to the rear, from "Private Peat," by Harold Peat

A SIMPLE PLAN/ GO BADGERS

So here's the problem:
Once blood's shed
there's no going back
So here's the Wisconsin Plan
from a Canadian English Lit prof
at the University of Wisconsin
Julia Grace Wales
who took her ideas to
European governments in 1917:

Nutshell?
Continuous mediation by smart people/
from neutral countries who listen/
to delegates from 'belligerent' countries
to mediate an end to the barbarities of war/
Keep listening /
keep talking /
 'til it's done
Not a bad strategy for life
when you think of it
{President Wilson liked it but
the sinking of the Lusitania
aroused public opinion
& the U.S. entered
the 'Great War' in 1917
& helped end it
So there's that}

Quebec native Julia Grace Wales was the great-granddaughter of the first paper mill owner in Canada. The McGill grad had a masters from Radcliffe. She taught at the University of Wisconsin, the University of London and the University of Cambridge (England). She co-authored a book of poetry, *Argenteuil Lyrics*, with her mother & sister. Her book *Democracy Needs Education* was published in 1942.

PHOTO: Julia Grace Wales /public domain

NOT AN EASY THING/MAURICE BRACEWELL

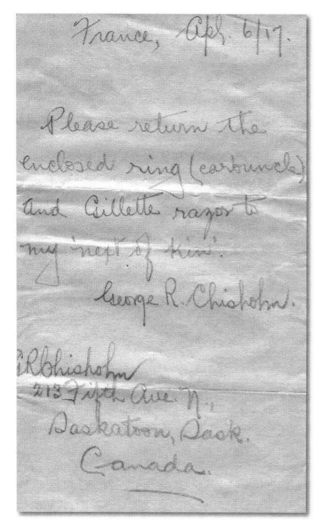

"Not an easy thing
Not a thing you soon forget
Going around among
friends of the day before
lying there face up
in all manner of grotesque shapes
Not a thing you soon forget

Not an easy thing
Not a thing you soon forget
watching Fritz blowing up
coal-mines in his back areas
When my partner suddenly crumples
falling at my feet
shot over the heart by a sniper
Not a thing you soon forget

Not an easy thing
Not a thing you soon forget
Hearing the shells whistling overhead
Easter Monday morning
the barrage-curtain falls
turning the whole of Vimy Ridge
into one exploding hell
Not a thing you soon forget" [20]

---

[20] This poem combines excerpts from the memoir of Maurice Wilfred Bracewell. He enlisted in Vancouver in 1915. He fought at Vimy Ridge and Passchendaele, where he was wounded. He died in Vancouver in 1973. Letters courtesy canadianletters.ca / VIU

ABOVE: George R. Chisholm's last will & testament. The Pictou, Nova Scotia native & Saskatoon resident wrote the note just before dying at Vimy Ridge / CanadianLetters.ca

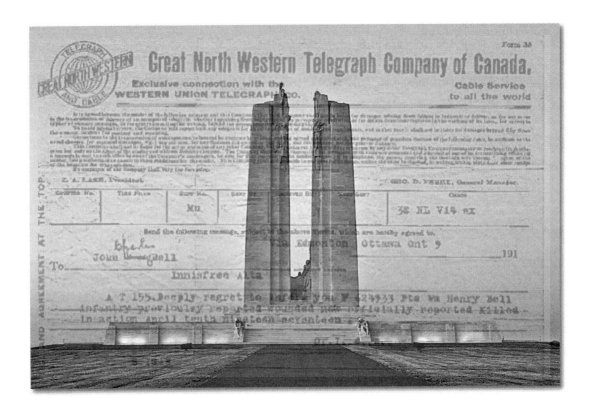

WHEN HE LOOKS AT HILL 145/AT VIMY

He sees tunnels/He sees diggers
Canadian boys/making ready for the battle
He sees youth
Standing at the heights/its view of the Douai Plain for miles
He sees strategic importance in a war dragged on for years
He sees weak rock & chalk/he sees havoc among men
He hears explosives/he feels the impact of shells on earth
He sees determination/he sees the creeping barrage/the footsteps
He sees it from their shoes/He sees sacrifice
when he looks at Hill 145/at Vimy

PHOTO by Geerhard Joos: The Canadian National Vimy Memorial, lit up at dusk, / photo illustration by J. Carmichael. News of son William Henry Bell's death at Vimy Ridge came by telegram to his father John Charles Bell. Telegram courtesy CanadianLetters.ca
Based on an interview with Marc & Patricia Betournay at the site of the Vimy Canadian National Memorial in France. Marc was Canada's chief engineer. The inscription at the site of Canada Bereft reads: "Head bowed in sorrow, she provides a powerful representation of Canada, a young nation grieving her dead. Overlooking the Douai Plain, she gazes down upon a symbolic tomb draped in laurel branches and bearing a helmet and sword."

VIMY KNOWS

Vimy knows
What it costs/This brilliant plan/The creeping barrage
100,000 Canadians pouring over Vimy Ridge/
infantrymen creeping carefully
in the near wake of artillery onslaught from 850 Canadian cannon
A model of Canadian ingenuity/What the French & British couldn't do alone
Taking trench after trench/This relentless Easter push that scars her earth
-the main height/Hill 145 & the top part so fetchingly described as "The Pimple"
What does it cost? Vimy knows
Life for 3,600 men/Grief for 3,600 families
Loss & rehabilitation for 5,000 wounded/Solace of angels be with them
The costs were greater than the sum of all these casualties
If growing up is the death of fairy tales
For Canada this happened in 1917 at Vimy/
where Canada was brilliant
The protest song wonders/
Where have all the flowers gone?
Vimy knows/She can see them from here

PHOTO by Steven Van Den Eynde: A view of Canada Bereft from the Canadian National Vimy Monument /
photo illustration Brad K. Larson

SIG SECTION & TRENCH MORTAR

His job:
Pop up
Signal back
In semaphore
to the artillery

///

Pop up
Signal back
In semaphore
to the artillery

///

A sniper's bullet gores this
pocket journal
piercing father's hopes for his son
"From your father with wishes
for a speedy return & season's greetings"

Forever a teen at Vimy Ridge

| Pte. Roger Irving | age 17 | penned: |
| "Sept. 5 1917 | — sig section" & | "trench mortar" |

— — —

So very young / He did what his country asked of him

Under white stone	His family will find him	midst thousands in a wheatfield
at Vimy Ridge where	immaculate graves/	a flower at every marker/
are tended daily/	tenderly/	with thanks / in France

Bullet-pierced journal of Pte. Roger Irving, photo courtesy Bill Irving

KINDNESS BLOOMS

Kindness blooms
In angst-filled rooms
amidst bedpans
thermometers
needles & urinals
sheets & scalpels
midnight watches
fevered brows
unmended bones
broken nerves
damaged lungs
blood & sweat & tears
Amidst all that/
In war's deep gloom
Kindness blooms
Humour unfolds
In an autograph book
like paper poppies
from grateful
wounded soldiers
where battle looms
Kindness blooms

Photo: English/
Canadian nurse
Emmeline Sears
Davidson
& cartoon done by
a recovering soldier
on a page in her
autograph book
at Wimereux in
Pas de Calais, France
Photo & image courtesy
CanadianLetters.ca / VIU

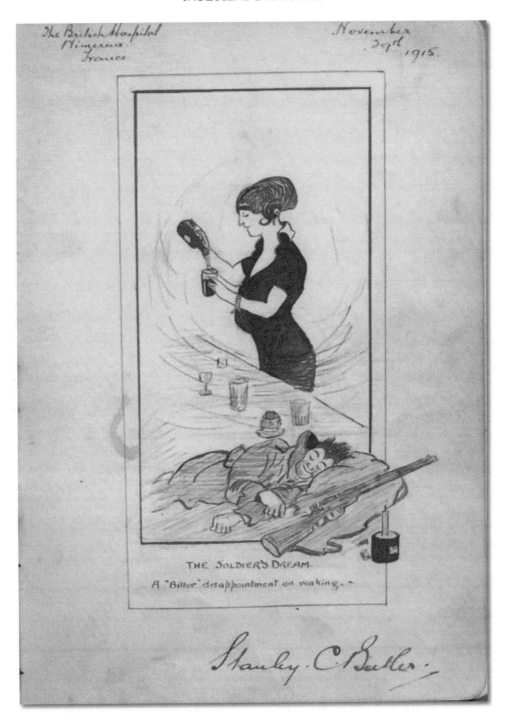

Cartoon done by a recovering soldier on a page in the autograph book of English/
Canadian nurse Emmeline Sears Davidson at Wimereux in Pas de Calais, France.

Image courtesy CanadianLetters.ca

MISERY ☹ & HUMOUR ☺

n the trench about a foot or two
from the bottom
there is a step against the parapet
on which men stand to fire /
Along this lay, sound asleep,
many of the poor fellows/
It was raining & they were vainly
trying to cover both head & feet
with the rubber sheet ...

... I heard a good louse story yesterday
A Tommy found a louse in his moustache
He picked it off &
holding it up said
'What a deserter eh,
Go back to the barracks'
So saying he opened his shirt
& tucked it in"[21]

-Maj. Rev. William Beattie

---

[21] ABOVE PHOTO: Maj. Rev. William Beattie as chaplain, CanadianLetters.ca.
A natural response to stress for some, humour cheered & relieved tension at the front & was seen as a morale builder in a grim era. Comedy shows were brought to places like Poperinge, Belgium's Talbot House where soldiers let off steam. Maj. Rev. William Beattie, minister at the Presbyterian Church in Cobourg, enlisted and became senior chaplain to the Second Division. His letters (such as this one) were often published in the Cobourg World Newspaper. He was created a Commander of St. Michael and St. George in recognition of "...his most conspicuous gallantry and distinguished conduct at the gas attack at St. Julien and through all the subsequent severe fighting of the period. Working unremittingly, with complete disregard to danger, he assisted in collecting wounded on many fields of action." He later returned to Ottawa in 1918 to organize the Chaplain Service of Canada and was promoted to the rank of Colonel. Non-combatants, 179 British chaplains were killed while ministering in World War 1.

PHOTO by Andy Wright:

Trench humour near Prowse Point Military Cemetery, France. "Charing Cross (London) 105 miles/< that way ... Victoria Cross (medal, often awarded posthumously) 20 yards > that way (pointing to No Man's Land)

HAIKU: ANYTHING FOR A LAUGH

Gallows humour
Trench humour/Same thing
Keep on/sunny side

"Always Look On the
Bright Side of Life" - Monty Python
Great medicine/Laughter

How would the joke go, again?
"A German, an Austro-Hungarian, a Belgian, a Serbian, a Frenchman,
A Briton, a Canadian, a South African, an American, an Italian, a Russian, an Indian, a Japanese man, a
Thai man, an Australian, and an {insert nationality here}
all walk into a war ...."

UNFINISHED MELODY FOR A LUTHIER

Play him a lullaby/
Play him a song/
Play that sweet vibrato
Let it emanate from gleaming wood
For men who fought a war someone else started/
& Richard Spencer Howard helped to finish
For generations the instrument he started
rested in pieces

Awaiting assembly/
Awaiting strings/
Awaiting destiny
One of countless pieces of creativity
halted by the war
A century later someone took notice
Now the world knows a violin
Richard Spencer Howard started/
someone else would finish
And it still sings/
So play him a lullaby
to rest in peace[22]

---

[22] PHOTO by Paul Chapman: A Leeds, England luthier envisioned a violin in 1915. Richard Spencer Howard signed & dated its wafer thin parts & left for war. He died at the Battle of Messines in 1917. Many decades later, Oxford luthier Roger Claridge put the violin together. Musician Sam Sweeney, violinist of the group Bellowhead, purchased the newly assembled antique & his father Chris Sweeney then wrote a book about it all: *Richard Spencer Howard: The Man Who Made Violins*. Upon learning more about her grandfather through the violin's revival, his granddaughter Mary Sterry wrote a note and left it on his grave. In the visitors' book, she wrote: "His fiddle still sings."

EXCERPTED JOURNALS/JAMES A. JONES, RICHDALE, ALBERTA

Front line, Heavy shell fire, terrible experience. Too bad this thing must continue. {"Thursday, April 26th , 1917}

Friday, April 27th, 1917 – In support of dugout, brick yard Fritz dropping heavies over on top of us. Appear to be in danger of death all the time.

Sunday, April 29th, 1917 – Day opens quietly. 1st 2nd + 3rd Divisions have gone over the top. Our turn next. Lord help us.

Friday, May 4th, 1917 – Got three lovely letters from Fannie, I am glad I have such a good wife, God grant I may be spared to return to her again.

Friday, May 11th, 1917 – Relieved ten o'clock at night. Jimmy gets lost and spends night in bush under shell fire.

Friday, May 18th, 1917 – Sports in afternoon. Feel blue as I think of return to trenches. I want to see the dear old home again.

Wednesday, May 23rd, 1917 – Our last day in Reserve. Wonder if I will live to come out again. "War is hell" said General Sherman and I wonder what would be his thoughts if he could see this one.

Saturday, June 2, 1917 – In supports and due to go over the top on Sunday morning. This may be my last entry if among those who fall. I die firm in the belief of a crucified Christ. I want my wife to know that my only regret was on her account and die blessing her with my last breath. May God protect her."

{His wife Fanny made the final notation, with underlines.}
Friday, June 29, 1917 – "The day my darling died. Gone but never forgotten"

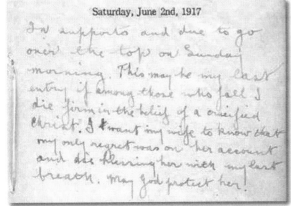

HOW TO BURY A MAN AT SEA

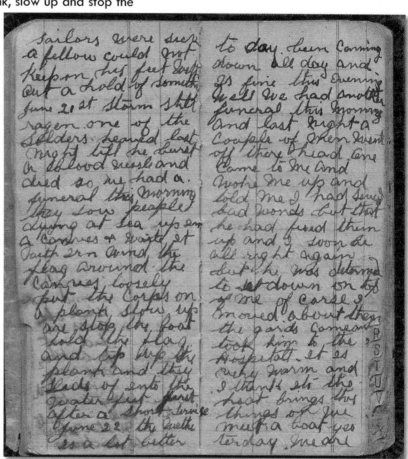

Storm still ragin' ... One of the soldiers heaved last night till he burst a blood vessel and died so we had a funeral this morning ...

They sew people dying at sea up in a canvas and weight it with iron and wrap the flag around the canvas loosely, put the corpse on a plank, slow up and stop the boat, hold the flag & tip up the plank & they slide off into the water, but first ... a short service

June 22... Well we had another funeral this morning and last night a couple of men went off their head / One came to me and woke me up and told me I had several bad wounds but that he had fixed them up and I would soon be all right again, but he was determined to set down on top of me / Of course I moved ... about then the guards came and took him to the hospital/It is very warm

and I think the heat brings these things on"[23] —

Allan Matheson Conquergood

[23] Allan Matheson Conquergood was a native of Kincardine, Ontario. His parents lived in Lillyfield, Manitoba. He enlisted in 1916, with the 239th Battalion's Railway Construction Corps. Conquergood had his right thumb and first two fingers amputated after an accident in 1898. A doctor declared him fit to serve, noting he wrote very well with his remaining little finger and ring finger. Conquergood served in Mesopotamia, discharged on 30 May 1919. Photos/1917 journal excerpt courtesy CanadianLetters.ca/VIU

Canada Post stamp designed by Lara Minja of Lime Design / Illustration Dennis Budgen

STAMP OF HONOUR

Who will cut these trees? Build this road?
Lay that track? Sling this bridge?
Defuse these mines? Take away these bodies? Dig that trench?
The recruiter turns you away from the recruiting station
The recruiter doesn't see your Canadian-ness {which is the same as his}
He sees only the tone of your skin {which he sees not the same as his}
Come 1915, Canadian enlistees "couldn't" be refused on account of race

Some commanders welcome black volunteers who stand/fight/fall
at Vimy & Passchendaele with their peers/Others not so much
In 1915 Lt.-Col. George Fowler, 104th Battalion shows just how far Canada has to go in civil rights
when he tries to discharge 20 black soldiers for their colour
"I have been fortunate to have secured a very fine class of recruits/
and I did not think it fair to these men that they should have to mingle with
Negroes," he wrote

Though discrimination is entrenched {so to speak} the British need all hands on
deck / No. 2 Construction Battalion/CEF
Canada's first/last/only segregated battalion is formed
Chaplain Capt. Rev. William A White is the only
black commissioned officer in the CEF
{compared to 600 in the U.S. forces}
The No. 2 Construction Battalion works 6 days a week/10 hours a day/
logging/tracklaying/with hand tools/in bleak condition/in segregated tents
Cut these trees! Build this road! Lay that track! Sling this bridge!
Defuse these mines! Take away these bodies! Dig that trench!
The recruiter will see you now!
Your nation will recognize your service late
A 2014 postage stamp hails the No. 2 Construction Battalion

PHOTOS: TOP RIGHT, Rev. William A. White. Raised in Nova Scotia, he is the only black commissioned officer in the CEF. BELOW: Members of the No. 2 Construction Battalion CEF/public domain

SALUTE TO BILLY BISHOP

Want to be like Billy! Billy Bishop, Victoria Cross recipient
His citation published 11 Aug 1917 in the *London Gazette*
A walking/flying TED talk! How motivational are his award citations!
For destroying an astounding 72 enemy planes
& leading in the air & on the ground he received

The Distinguished Flying Cross:
"His value as a moral factor to the Royal Air Force
cannot be over-estimated"
The Distinguished Service Order:
"His courage and determination have
set a fine example to others"
The Distinguished Service Order Bar:
"His consistent dash and great fearlessness have set a magnificent example
to the pilots of his squadron" & "on all occasions displaying a fighting spirit
and determination to get to close quarter with his opponents"
Add to these the Legion d'Honeur &
The Croix de Guerre with Palm
What is often overlooked about Billy Bishop:

At school he was known for fighting
He was not a great student/
he was easily discouraged
He repeated a year for cheating
And yet: this classic underachiever found his bliss & went on to great success
There's a lake named for William Avery Bishop in the Northwest Territories
A smash play & TV adaptation
A park in Ottawa/A mountain in Alberta/A Legion branch in Vancouver
A hazardous materials training centre at CFB Borden
A hangar in Brampton/An entrance at a Hamilton school
A trophy with the Air Force Association
A squadron of the Royal Canadian Air Cadets in Owen Sound
A building at the 1st Canadian Air Division
& Canadian NORAD Region HQ in Winnipeg & an airport in Toronto
& the ultimate compliment: A Canada Post stamp
So there's hope for me & you yet
Be like Billy!

YORKSHIRE TO YPRES

"The larks still bravely singing fly, scarce heard among the guns below"
— Lt. Col. Dr. John McCrae

So many stones/So many poppies
A quilt of graves of men & boys here
but quietly women served/died
Staff Nurse Nellie Spindler/one of just two women
buried in military cemeteries in Belgium[24]

---

[24] As hell unfurled like an enemy flag Staff Nurse Nellie Spindler enlisted with the Queen Alexandra's Imperial Military Nursing Service. She expertly treated urgent abdominal chest & thigh wounds at the No. 44 clearing station at Brandhoek. It was 7 miles from front lines but not out of range of German shells aiming for our munitions. A friend said Nellie knew they were all in danger, but her letters home were full of cheer. She never saw the exploding shell that sent a large piece of shrapnel through her back. Her nurse's watch stilled forever 21 Aug 1917. On the casualty form for officers she was listed as killed in action. She was one of just two women in one of the largest Commonwealth graveyards, she was buried at Lijssenthoek with full military honours and the Last Post. The Director of Medical Services of the Army & the Surgeon General attended her funeral. Her grave is one of the most decorated and visited at the Lijssenthoek cemetery.

PHOTO by J. Carmichael/ illustration Brad K. Larson: Poppies & crosses at the grave of Staff Nurse Nellie Spindler at Lijssenthoek

WE BRING THESE SEVEN PEBBLES

Seven pebbles to remember
Small solid stones
Reminders to truly
rest in peace
Seven pebbles
On an altar / like your life
Not fleeting / like breath
But lasting / like memory
Enduring / like souls
Seven pebbles to remember

PHOTO by J. Carmichael : Grave of Abraham (Slobodinsky) Slowe of the King's Own Yorkshire Regiment, with stones left as traditional Jewish gestures of respect /At Lijssenthoek Cemetery/ according to jewsfwwlondon.com, "He had a great sense of his duty & he carried it out to the last," wrote his commanding officer, W. Scott Hill, in a note to Slowe's mother

POPERINGE

Hops for that Belgian beer were probably
born in Poperinge/Pop for short
In the Great War/one of the rare places
to get a good night's sleep
One of just two towns in Belgium
not under German occupation
Eight miles/a long way from Ypres
A safe place to billet British troops
& for field hospitals
& an R&R getaway for the war-weary/
Talbot House/an oasis then & now
You can still get a hospitable cuppa
midst the loveliness of cobbled streets
Residents historically famed for stubbornness/
dubbed "cobble-heads"
Great War reminders remain a century later
Two death cells in the town hall
& a public execution post
Nearby at Lijssenthoek
Thousands of soldiers sleep forever

PHOTOS/J. Carmichael: Talbot House sign &
Statue designed by Nele Boudry recalling Eliane
"Ginger" Cossey, a girl who worked at La Poupee Café.

THE WAR NEEDS FEET/FEET NEED BOOTS

A scrap of harness leather here /
couple stitches — so — snip!
a few nails for that heel — there
Left one's good as new almost
if you see Fritz give 'im the boot /
try to keep it out of the shell holes will you?
Sidelined {oddly enough} by my FEET/trenchfoot
I could not keep up on the march;
With my Lewis gun skills they wanted to put me for a flyboy's gunner
Terrible life expectancy those flyboys
I have watched them fall right out of the sky & break apart
I'm happy *the trainer didn't keep his appointment*
It turns out that some of the skills I learned watching my father
cobble up shoes for neighbourhood children in Oklahoma & Alberta come in handy
The saddler & an armorer & a farrier & me are a little mobile work crew /
Turned into a group of technicians /
I'm hobbling fireside cooking/limping & cobbling boots
Good thing that I can cook &/fix shoes/ & limp
Good thing the war needs feet
Feet need boots
Boots just might save my life

PHOTO
by Lies Depuydt:
from WOI Living
History at Museum
Weekend in
Zonnebeke,
Belgium

COUNT THE COST

Tell me/proper/blunt/the price
Not the statistics
Not the number of casualties
Tell me in an epitaph
Tell me on Portland stone
what he might have said/
for there is hardly a
better single measure of loss
14 words to gauge
the visceral nature of grief
Engrave it in Cree/
what he might have said/
Tell me what J Chookomolin/
age 22/
might have said
He served as 2497978 Private J. Jakomolin /
Canadian Forestry Corps
He died 20 Sept 1917

According to findagrave.com, his inscription in Cree syllabics reads:
iKina-ka-ta-o Ta-ni-s Ne-s-ta Ni-wi-ka-ma-ka-n Na-meh-ko-si-pi-k O-ma Ma-shi-keh-wi-ni-k O-chii   /

"I left my wife and daughter
at Nahmehkoo Seepee (Trout River)
for   this   War,"

he might have said

PHOTO by Ian Fletcher: Pte. J. Chookomolin's grave at Lijssenthoek.

'SNOWFLAKE': CONSCIENTIOUS OBJECTOR

Voracious/the war monster must have bodies
Voluntary enlistment turns into the draft
Conscientious objectors mocked as
unmanly/called anything BUT conscientious
Imagined as a ridiculous cartoon
Considered the "Snowflake" of his day
Shiny patent dress boots! An eiderdown quilt in
his blanket roll! A baby soother close at hand! A
hot water bottle nearby!
Tea & sweets & insect powder
ever handy in pockets!
Handfuls exempted for religious inclination:
Quaker/Mennonite/Doukhobor
Some exempted for critical occupation
Some resisting the call to arms in light of
horrific casualty rates
Absence of a uniform frequently brought
shaming/delivery of a white feather/
hostilities/mocking/bullying from some whose
husbands & brothers were at the Front
Those who will fight are pressured to scorn those
who won't fight
The degree of resistance determined official
treatment/Many were subject to brutality/
hard labour/prison
Some stood in harm's way/
treating the wounded on frontlines
with the Friends Ambulance
{others grimly concluding that as medics/
they were enabling war}

image courtesy CanadianLetters.ca /VIU A
soldier's art from the wartime-autograph book of
English Nurse Emmeline Sears Davidson

SAY, YOUNG MAN!

What would it take?
How do you get men to fight?
When the word is out on
war's brutality/The carnage wrought
The blood-bathed forests/the never-
ending lists of the KIA/MIA/DOW
{killed in action/missing in action/
died of wounds}
{not to mention poison gas}
The decimation of an entire
generation
How do you get them to leave their
warm cozy homes in St. Catherine's?
How do you get them to pick up
a bayonet & use it
Rumours of Hun savagery will help
of course/Propaganda's the ticket!
Something unprovable about
a Canadian crucified on a barn door
But how do you really
apply the thumbscrews?
Put a bounty out for new recruits
maybe ... Shame seems to work for
a lot of things/Ah/good/you've
covered that with "sit back in shame'
Drop the C-word — Call them Cowards in a good cop/bad cop way
"I know you're not yella!" "Who you callin' yella??"
Urge them to "Be British!" "Play the man!"
Is offering "comradeship & protection of men from
your own city" a veiled threat? If so/that might work ...
Will men from my own city come get me if I don't enlist?
If all else fails/appeal to their fashion sense
- the latest & best style of clothes is khaki!
{& it goes really well with RED}
Get it on and show your *manhood*! Say, Young Man!
We'd like to think these wouldn't work today/
100 years later
Shiver to wonder/what would it take?

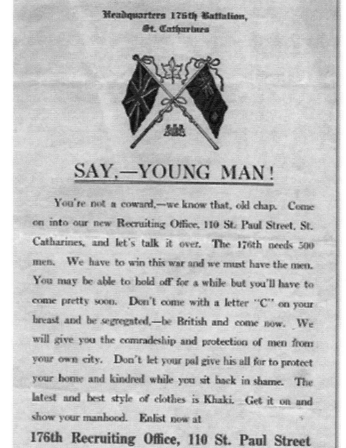

FOUND HAIKU/SHOT AT DAWN

PHOTOS by Geerhard Joos: From the gravestones of Shot At Dawn soldiers: clockwise from top right, E.S. Poole, S. Stewart, A.H. Westwood, F. Turner J. Steadman.

SHOT AT DAWN/THE STAKES

The number: 309 Commonwealth soldiers {boys some of them/young as 14}
{25 Canadians} ordered to be executed by their superiors
The punishment: Shot at dawn/No legal representation/No military honours/
No proper marker/No pension
The crimes {Yes, these are considered crimes}: Leaving the battle/Putting down a gun/Leaving the
trench to warm up/Sleeping on the job
The justification: "Desertion"/Cowardice" "Every man essential" "An example"
The problem: In retrospect most desertions can be attributed to PTSD/combat stress/medical
illness/even a hearing disorder/so the executions come across as barbaric
The compounding: Families shamed/Mothers with no pensions/Fatherless children
The added grief: Soldiers/officers forced to shoot their fellows
The holdouts: Australia/the U.S. would not execute their "disgraced" soldiers
The pardons: In 2000 Canadian Parliament put names of 25 executed soldiers
on the Roll of Honour / better late than never but the shame lingers as long as their memories

SHOT AT DAWN (S.A.D.)

Pte Abigail J H /Pte Adamson J S /Labourer Ahmed M M / Pte Ainley G / Sgt Alexander W /. Pte Allsop A E / Pte Anderson J A / Pte Anderson W / Pte Ansted A T / Pte Archibald J / Pte Arnold F S / L/Sgt Ashton H / L/Cpl Atkinson A / Pte Auger F /Pte Baker W / Pte Ball J / Pte Barker W / Pte Barnes J E / Rfn Barratt F M / Pte Bateman F / Pte Bateman J /Pte Beaumont E A /Sapper Beeby E /Dvr Bell J / Rfn Bellamy W /Pte Benham W / Pte Bennett J / Pte Black P / Pte Bladen F C H / Pte Blakemore D J / Pte Bolton E / Pte Botfield A / Pte Bowerman W /Pte Brennan J / Pte Briggs A / Pte Briggs J / Pte Brigham T / Pte Britton C / Pte Broadrick F / Pte Brown A / Pte Brown A / Pte Bryant E / Pte Burden H F / Pte Burrell W H / Pte Burton R / Pte Butcher F C / Pte Byers J / Pte Byrne S / Monaghan M / Pte Cairnie W / Pte Cameron J / Pte Card E A / Pte Carey J / Pte Carr J / Pte Carter H G / Pte Carter H / Pte Cassidy J / Pte Chase H / Rfn Cheeseman F W / Pte Clarke H A / Pte Clarke W / Pte Collins G / Pte Comte G / Pte Crampton J / Pte Crimmins H / Pte Crozier J / Pte Cummings T / Pte Cunnington S / Pte Cuthbert J / Pte Cutemore G / Pte Dalande H / Pte Davis R M / Pte Davis T / Pte Degasse A C / Pte DeLargey E / Pte DeLisle L / Pte Dennis J J / Pte Depper C / Pte Docherty J / Pte Docherty T / Rfn Donovan T / Rfn Donovan T / Pte Dossett W / Pte Downey P / Pte Downing T /

Pte Elford L / Pte Evans A / Pte / Pte Fatoma A / Pte Fellows E / Pte / Pte Fox J / L/Cpl Fox J S V / Pte Pte Gibson D / Pte Giles P / Sgt Graham J / Pte Haddock A J / Dvr G / Rfn Harding F / Pte Harris E W / Pte Hart B / Pte Hartells H H / Dvr Pte Hendricks H / Pte Higgins J / Pte L/Cpl Holland J / Pte Holmes A / Pte Horler E / Pte Hughes F / L/Cpl Hughes Hunter W / Rfn Hyde J J / Pte Ingham Pte Jackson E / Pte Jeffries A L / Pte Pte Jones R M / Pte Jones W / Gunner King J / Pte Kirk E / Pte Kirman C H / Dvr Lamb A / Cpl Latham G / Pte / Pte Ling W N / Pte Loader F / Pte MacDonald H / Cpl MacDonald J / A / Pte Martin H / Pte Mayers J / Rfn Rfn McCracken J E / Pte McCubbin B / Pte Michael J S / Pte Milburn J B / Pte Mitchell L / Pte Moles T L / Pte Mullany J / Pte Murphy H T / Pte Murray R / Pte Neave W / Pte Nelson B / Pte O'Neill F / Pte O'Neill A / Pte R G / Pte Penn M / Pte Perry E / Pte Poole E S / Pte Poole H / Cpl Povey G Reynolds E J / Pte Richmond M R / Pte Roberts W W / Sgt Robins J J / Pte Roe G E / Pte Rogers J / Drummer Rose Pte Scholes W / Pte Scotton W / Pte Sims R W / Pte Siniski D / Pte Skilton C Rfn Smith J / Pte Smith W / Pte Smith / Pte Spry W T / Pte Stead F / Pte

Sub Lt Dyett E (RNVR) / Pte Earl W / Pte Earp A G / Eveleigh A / Pte Everill G / Pte Fairburn E / Pte Farr H Ferguson J / Pte Flynn H / Pte Foulkes T / Pte Fowles S Frafra A / Pte Fraser E / Pte Fryer J / Pte Gawler R / Gleadow G E / L/Cpl Goggins P / Pte Gore F C / Pte Hamilton T G / Pte Hamilton/Blanchard A / Pte Hanna Pte Harris L / Pte Harris T / Pte Harris /Bevistein A / Hasemore J W / Pte Hawkins T / L/Cpl Hawthorne F / Higgins J M / Pte Highgate T J / Pte Hodgetts O W / Holt E / Pte Hope R / Pte Hope T / Pte Hopkins T / Pte G E / Pte Hughes J / Pte Hunt W / Pte Hunter G / Pte A / Rfn Irish/Lee G / L/Cpl Irvine W J / Cpl Ives F / Jennings J / Pte Johnson F/Charlton J / Pte Jones J T / Jones/Fox W / Pte Kerr H H / Pte Kershaw J / Pte Pte Knight H J / Pte LaLancette J / Pte LaLiberte C / Lawrence E A / Cpl Lewis C / Pte Lewis G / Pte Lewis J Lodge H E J / Pte Longshaw A / Pte Lowton G H / Pte Pte Mackness E / Sapper Malyon F / L/Cpl Mamprusi McBride S / Pte McClair H/Rowland / Pte McColl C F / Pte McFarlane J / Pte McGeehan B / Pte McQuade J / Milligan C M / Pte Mills G / Pte Mitchell A / Pte Molyneaux J / L/Cpl Moon W A / Pte Morris H / Dvr Murphy A / Pte Murphy P / Pte Murphy W / Pte W B / Pte Nicholson C B / Pte Nisbet J / Pte O'Connell Palmer H / Rfn Parker A E / Pte Parry A / Pte Pattison Phillips L R / Pte Phillips W T H / Pte Pitts A / 2nd. Lt H / Pte Randle W H / Cpl Reid J / Pte Reid I / Pte Rickman A / Pte Rigby T H B / Pte Roberts J W / Pte Robinson A H / Pte Robinson J / Pte Robinson W / Pte F / Pte Sabongida S / Pte Salter H / L/ Cpl Sands P / Seymour J / Pte Sheffield F / Pte Simmonds W H / Pte W F / Pte Slade F W / Pte Sloane J / Pte Smith J C / W / Pte Smythe A / Dvr Spencer J / Pte Spencer V M Steadman J B / Pte Stevenson D / Pte Stevenson R / Pte

Stewart S / L/Sgt Stones J W / Pte Swain J / Dvr Swaine J W / Trooper Sweeney J J / Pte Tanner E / Pte Taylor J / Pte Taylor J / Pte Taysum N H / Rfn Templeton J / Pte Thomas J / Pte Thompson A D / Pte Thompson W L / Pte Tite R T / Pte Tongue J / Pte Troughton A / Pte Turner F / Pte Turpie W J / Sgt Wall J T / L/Sgt Walton W / Pte Ward G / Pte Ward T / Pte Watkins G / Pte Watts T W / Pte Watts W / Pte Webb H J / Pte Welsh C / Pte Westwood A H / Pte Wild A / Pte Williams H / Pte Wilson J H / Cpl Wilton J / Pte Wishard J / Rfn Woodhouse J / Pte Worsley E / Pte Wright F / Pte Wycherley W / Rfn Yeoman W / Pte Young E / Pte Young R.

PHOTO by Nora Platt: Shot at Dawn Memorial / National Memorial Arboretum, Staffordshire, UK / designed by sculptor Andy deComyn / modelled after 17-year-old Pte. Herbert Burden, a volunteer, who was shot for desertion. These are the names of the Commonwealth soldiers executed/shot at dawn during World War I.

BLACK JACK/DOBBSY & THE SRD

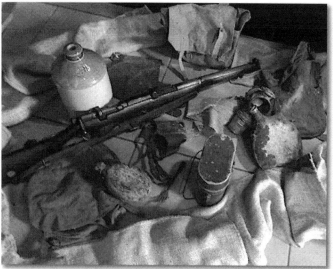

Where's the rum, Dobbsy?
Where's the SRD, pal?
I wish I could ask Dobbs where the rum is
He was toting the section's ration of
Supply Reserve Depot/Service Rum Diluted
Seldom Reaches Destination/Soon Runs Dry
1/16th of a pint per man per day:
to be dispensed at the front daily at stand-to
when he was hit & that's the last we saw of it
Wherever you are, Dobbsy
- God love you –
Don't go to hell/
It's sure to be overrun with rats, lice,
& a Tommy at every fire
to keep Fritzy sizzling

LETTER HOME/ON DRINK

I am glad to say that I have quit drinking water since I have left the trenches where we get a little rum. We get good tea 3 times a day/the water is not much good. A person cannot say that he drinks rum. You do not get a drink, only a swallow. It will strangle you quicker than white-wine vinegar if you go to take a breath between the two little swallows why your wind has gone for the time being. But it cheers one up wonderfully after being up all night with nothing to eat to see the sergeant coming up the trench with the rum in a water bottle under his arm. We are always willing to wait a few minutes longer to get our issue. If you ever hear anybody say that they think it's a shame that the soldiers are given rum, why just tell them a thing or two from me. I'll bet they don't have any boys over here they don't know under what conditions we have to live over here."

-   *Lawrence Earl Johns of Elimville, Ont. died September 12, 1917. – courtesy CanadianLetters.ca*

DIARY ENTRY – WHEN TO IMBIBE/WEDNESDAY SEPTEMBER 6, 1916

This morning we were wakened up for a ration of rum. Of course as per promise to Gussie I passed it by as I was not in necessity. The rum is really an emergency ration served out when the men are wet or extra tired, of after an engagement or a heavy shelling when nerves are badly shaken..."

-   *George Hedley Kempling, Toronto, Ont. Courtesy CanadianLetters.ca / VIU*

PHOTO by Lies Depuydt: An SRD jug amidst soldier's kit

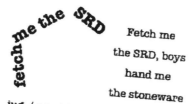

Fetch me
the SRD, boys
hand me
the stoneware
jug / a swig of Service Rum Diluted for us / after all

them trenches we dug / slogging through the trenches / wishing
we were home / in the company of the SRD / we are never alone
they say SRD stands for something else / as it Seldom Reaches
Destination / it's SRD for me boys / just give me my fair ration

It's back to Canada for those of us left / our days as soldiers all
through / I'm home with my folks and some bad memories / i'll
no' be forgetting you / them were good old days as I've missed
though I didn't think so then / I'll miss it enough to just re-enlist
for SRD and the company of fightin' men / so hoist a pint for me
boys when you talk about days of old / when we gave Fritzy hell
and dug trenches so well and survived in those fields of gold

THE CASE FOR RUM

I t is hard for one to understand the need for such thing if one has not been in it and does not understand the conditions. But when one takes the infantry man in the front line waiting to go over the top, standing cold and wet with the mud halfway to his knees, and knowing exactly that at the end of a few minutes he will be called upon to face the most fiendish and effective instruments of destruction that modern science has been able to invent, from the fifteen inch shell to the Mills bomb, from liquid fire to gas, one cannot help thinking that a shot of rum which for the meantime makes them feel warm even if in reality they are not any warmer and which for a time makes them forget in part the horrors they have to face, is a good thing for them." - *Harold Henry Simpson* / PEI [25]

A FRIEND TODAY/BUT NOT ALWAYS

Where were the detox programs when the soldiers returned
The dependence deemed so essential for making it through the war would prove
crippling for many after Armistice

---

[25] Harold Henry Simpson, Bayview, Prince Edward Island, enlisted in September, 1915, serving in France, Belgium, and Germany until his return to Canada. Letter courtesy CanadianLetters.ca

BLACK JACK/SHELL SHOCK

The worst?
The strain of waiting
for something to happen
Waiting for the slithering whistle of a shell
going higher then coming down
It's not an uncommon occurrence for men
 to go crazy under shell fire
The noise made by high explosive
makes your hair stand on end
The electricity of expectation
Along comes flying steel & fragments
The Front is just the place for
the person that likes thrills
Let me tell you about shell shock
It starts with cold chills & sinking stomach
Your brain urges your feet to beat it /
 but your feet won't move &
your knees get to wobbling
then your nerve breaks &
that's when you go bugs
I've seen it & it isn't nice

PHOTO by Andrew Mackay: Verdun Memorial

PHOTO by Robert Ward/ Public Domain: Cpl. Freddie Stowers' sisters, Georgina Palmer and Mary Bowens, with Barbara Bush and President George H.W. Bush at the Medal of Honor presentation ceremony 24 April 1991

BRAVE IS/CÔTE 188

Brave is Cpl. Freddie Stowers from Sandy Springs, South Carolina
Company C, U.S. 371st Infantry Regiment/Seconded to the French army
Brave is 28 Sept 1917/rising to lead a platoon in tatters
in an actual uphill battle/in the Ardennes/when your leaders have been gunned down
& your troops have been laid waste
Brave is reorganizing to go forward when the odds stack up hideous
against the determined few who remain & enfilade fire shreds your Plan B
Brave is leaning into machine gun fire because that's how to take the trench
& when you've been hit & your life is ebbing out/much like the war itself
Brave is that one final   push to   forge on
Brave is Cpl. Freddie Stowers from Sandy Springs, South Carolina[26]

---

[26] The French Army's Red Hand did take Côte 188 with Stowers' help. His recommendation for the Medal of Honour was officially misplaced, never processed until Congress asked the Department of the Army to investigate. 73 years after his death, his surviving sisters accepted the medal from President George H.W. Bush. Stowers Elementary on Fort Benning, Georgia and Corporal Freddie Stowers Single Soldier Billeting Complex on Fort Jackson, South Carolina are named in his honour. He is buried with his peers in the Meuse-Argonne American Cemetery & Memorial. America lost 116,708 lives in World War I.

OUT PAST THE ONIONS

Siol na fear fearail
Wide enough for two to walk/
or one to walk & one to pass
Spindly pan-handle hewn of neatly
manicured luxuriant lawn amidst
newly harvested fields of
Belgian root vegetables
The memorial to the Nova Scotia Highlanders
The Fighting 85th Canadian Infantry Battalion
Siol na fear fearail/Gaelic for "Breed of manly men"
A sharp left turn just past the onions
A solid stone monument put up
by the surviving peers of the Neverfails
A tribute to fallen brothers/
For the boys who were left
more terror followed/more valour ensued
Siol na fear fearail[27]

---

[27] Battle Honours for the Never Fails: Arras / Vimy / Ypres 1917 / Passchendaele / Scarpe 1918 / Amiens / Drocourt-Queant / Hindenburg Line / Canal du Nord / Valenciennes / Sambres / France & Flanders / {their first battle was capturing Hill 145 : in April 1917 they went over where the Vimy Memorial sits now} In October 1917 600 Neverfails fought to the bloody nub at Passchendaele. 600 went in/148 were killed/280 were wounded. 85 of the dead have no known grave. They are perpetuated by the Cape Breton Highlanders. PHOTO: J. Carmichael

EXCERPTS/LAST LETTER HOME FROM ALBERTA SOLDIER ALEX DeCOTEAU

My Dear Sister ... A man has lots of time to
think of his people and home out here,
and one does get awfully lonesome at times.
I know in my last trip to the front line,
I dreamed of home and "all the mothers, sisters
& sweethearts" I ever had ...
Most of the boys turn (fatalists)
They believe that everything is prearranged
by Divine Power, and if it one's time to die
no matter what one does, one has to die
Their motto is 'If my turn comes next,
I can't do anything to avoid it, so I should not worry'
They don't worry either
Of course there are lots who suffer from
shell shock or nervous breakdown, & they can't fight against fear, but most
of the boys have a keen sense of humor, and laugh at almost anything...

I am laying on the ground trying to finish this letter before dark/
I hope I do for I don't know when I'll have another opportunity ... [28]

-   *Alex De Coteau, France/10 Sept. 10, 1917*

PHOTO: Alex De Coteau in his running uniform public domain/LETTER courtesy canadianletters.ca/VIU PHOTO
ILLUSTRATION: Brad K. Larson

---

[28] Alexander Wuttunee DeCoteau of Eagle Hills/Battleford, #231462 49th Canadians, C.E.F. France, was Cree Canadian and the sole Albertan at the Stockholm Olympic Games in 1912. He took eighth place for Canada in the 5,000 metres. He was Canada's first Aboriginal police officer, joining the Edmonton police in 1911. He signed up for the CEF in 1915. King George V gave him his gold pocket watch for winning a five-mile race at Salisbury where he was training. Fleet of foot, he ran messages and guided troops through danger for two years/to the Second Battle of Passchendaele, where he was felled by the bullet of a German sniper on 30 Oct 1917. He was buried among 600 other Canadians on the Bellevue Spur. In 1985 members of the Cree community performed a ceremony in Edmonton to bring his spirit home to rest on the prairies. His short life lives on at several sports halls of fame, a park named for him at 105 Street & 102 Avenue in Edmonton & a residential area in south Edmonton named for him in 2014.

FULL CIRCLE IN 39 YEARS

You can go home again but you might have to stay
Migration from Europe to North America was reversed
for Richard Verhaeghe
Born in Ostend/Belgium
Husband of Augusta Verhaeghe of Saskatoon
A motorman for the street railway,

enlisted with his new country to
save his Old Country
Lance Corporal with the infantry
in the 5th Canadian Mounted Rifles
(Quebec Regiment)
In the grim battle
for Regina Trench
(the longest
German trench
of the war)
On 2 Oct 1916,
"he stayed behind
in the open and
dressed wounded,
being all the time
under extremely
heavy fire, rifle and
machine gun fire,
without any regard
for his own safety ...
He succeeded in getting
several of the wounded
into their own trench"

Lance Corp. Verhaeghe was Killed In Action 30 Oct 1917, age 39, just 48 km from where he was born/The only Belgian-Canadian known to be buried at Tyne Cot Cemetery, Belgium, Grave Location XXVIII. H.I. {in the Old Country}

PHOTO by J. Carmichael / PHOTO ILLUSTRATION: Brad K. Larson
Source: Veterans.gc.ca / Raoul Saesen

LANCE CPL. ROBERT ROLLO PAUL/ESCAPE FROM GERMAN POW CAMP

We were soon swallowed up in large tracks of bush and underbrush which grew denser until at last it became an almost impenetrable thicket. The words of Bunyan in describing the process of Christian up the Hill of Difficulty and afterwards through the Valley of the Shadow of Death could here be quoted almost without alteration. From running, we fell to going, and from going to crawling on our hands and knees. Frequently lost; frequently compelled to retrace the distance we had so painfully covered, inch by inch, ever endeavouring to keep our faces towards ... the distant North-West. We found ourselves in a swamp so boggy & interspersed with deep holes that we had to hold hands to avoid being quagmired ...

"In the deep darkness, drenched through and through, uncertain of our way, weary to the stage of acute pain, peevish to the extent of abusing one another, chilled in spine & to the point of resolving to give ourselves up to the first authorities, we crawled about for hours, until, just on the verge of complete exhaustion, we suddenly found ourselves in a farming country ...

"We met a man who accosted us and proved to be a Hun soldier equipped with pack, rifle and bayonet. He appeared to be in a hurry, but asked us for a light for a cigarette. This we were able to furnish him, and in return, he offered us each of "Belgia" cigarette, which we gratefully accepted. After he wished us a good evening and was proceeding on his way, it occurred to us to ask him what town we were approaching ... The information given by this good-natured German, no doubt home on leave from the Western front (and, after some refreshment in a beerhouse, too charitably disposed towards all men to trouble himself with our business) proved to be most valuable ...

"When we awoke and peeped from our hiding place we discovered to our dismay that a German sentry was at his post within a stone's throw of us. Waiting till night had fallen, we slipped down on the side away from the sentry ...

"Early on the eleventh night ... knowing that before morning we should be either in the land of freedom or again in the hands of the military authorities of Germany, doomed to days of imprisonment, starvation and cruelty, and, afterwards, to work far more severely than that of the slave at the galleys or in the cottonfields ... Our progress was sharply arrested by a sound which, in the words of Virgil, sent a shiver through our very bones. Directly in our path, and only a few yards away, stood a German sentry, endeavouring to keep circulation by stamping on the ground. If ever we had reason to bless the inclemency of the climate of Northern Europe which so frequently makes a man too intent upon his own discomforts to be keenly alive to outward sounds, it was then. Noiselessly, we retreated, then dropped to the ground and crawling around and past him. In so doing, I lost my friend, Paul, who was a little ahead and swallowed up in the darkness; so, after waiting a little while in the hope of finding him, I went on alone ...

"I saw a light appearing in a small house not far away ... I was able to get a glimpse of a middle-aged woman beginning her day's work. To my knock she responded with a "Who is there?" To which I replied somewhat evasively: "Am I in Holland?" Immediately, she partly opened the door and admitted me. Once inside, she assured me I was in Holland, but only a little way from the border. The road I had followed was leading me backwards toward the frontier ... her light had appeared just in time. The kind Dutch woman welcomed me very heartily and made me sit in a large armchair by a good fire and brought me a bowl of milk ... I was indeed in the land of freedom ... Such a luxury had been unthought of, unheard of, and unseen for almost a year and a half. Very soon I forgot my joys and fell fast asleep in my chair.

"When I awoke, the day was well advanced and I bade farewell to my kind hostess, who let me out as cautiously as she admitted me, and no wonder for out of the window, a few yards away, could be seen a German sentry guarding the frontier ...[29]

---

[29] Lance Corporal Robert R. Paul of Lavant, Ont. enlisted in Moose Jaw, Sask. With the 28th Battalion Machine Gun Section, CEF. He & Pte. W. Waters of the 2nd CMR's fell into German hands at Hooge, near Ypres, in June, 1916. After undergoing untold hardships for 17 months, they decided to stake all on a break for liberty. Pte. Waters also made it to freedom, & both men were returned to England. These excerpts from memoir, courtesy CanadianLetters.ca

PHOTO prior page: British War Medal issued to George Anderson "Black Jack" Vowel, courtesy Brian Vowel.

PASSCHENDAELE WOUNDS/25 Oct 1917

Amid the din of the bursting shells I called to Stephens, but got no response and just assumed he hadn't heard me. He was never seen or heard from again. He had not deserted. He had not been captured. One of those shells that fell behind me had burst and Stephens was no more ...

"A few paces ahead a shell hole on my right attracted my attention and horror. There was that curly-head face downwards on one side of the shell hole, and his body on the other. There was no time for grief or tenderness ... in another shell hole were two live Germans-but only just alive. They were mere boys and could not have been more than 16 years of age-both bleeding profusely but the look in their eyes I have never been able to forget ... abject fear mingled somehow with pity. I remember I hastily grabbed my water bottle, drank a sip and threw it to within their reach ... I felt a bang and toppled into a shell hole on my left. Chips who was on my right side yelled 'Oh, my wrist.' I quickly realised my left leg was useless and we had both been hit by the same bullet ...

It was just one stretch of water interspersed with rings of earth here and there which I knew were the edges of shell holes and I must keep out of them or drown ... How I kept my bearings I shall never know ... How long that quarter of a mile took me to traverse I do not know, but at last a friendly voice called 'Suds!' ... They and five more were all that were left of our 27. Shells fell all around us and none of us expected to reach the dressing station, only 300 yards away. It was four hours before we did reach it. The stretcher was full of water, mud and blood; at one halting I managed to slap a field dressing, dragged from the lining of my tunic, on to my knee to try and stop the bleeding. At long last we made it, and to me the very worst kind of hell upon earth was over ...

The enemy and ourselves were in the self-same muck, degradation and horror to such a point nobody cared any more about anything, only getting out of this, and the only way out was by death or wounding and we all of us welcomed either.[30] — *John Pritchard Sudbury*

---

[30] John Pritchard Sudbury of London County, Ontario, served with the 9th Canadian Brigade Machine Gun Company at Ypres, The Somme, and Vimy Ridge, until he was wounded at Passchendaele on 26 Oct 1917. Infected in the mud, his gangrenous leg was eventually amputated. 1963 memoir excerpts & photo courtesy CanadianLetters.ca / VIU

PTE. JAMES PETER ROBERTSON VC

When the chips are down
You will be first to volunteer/seize the gun/
save the day
When the snipers are badly wounded
You will carry them in one by one/
under severe fire
You will literally lay down your lif e
to save another
You shone
You shine still[31]

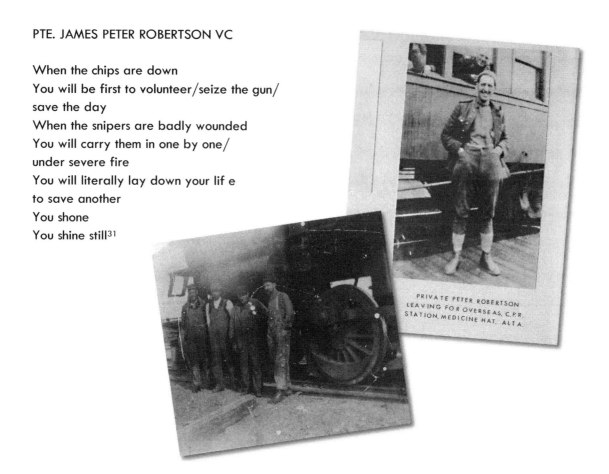

PRIVATE PETER ROBERTSON
LEAVING FOR OVERSEAS, C.P.R.
STATION, MEDICINE HAT, ALTA.

---

[31] There's a park and a street and a Canadian Coast Guard patrol vessel and a lake named for Pte. James Peter "Pete" Robertson / Victoria Cross. Born in Albion Mines, Nova Scotia, later a resident of Medicine Hat, Alberta, he was a CPR railway engineer known for his wonderful singing voice.

The call went out in the Corps on 6 Nov 1917 as they made their way to the Belgian village of Passchendaele - an actual uphill battle. "We need 27th Battalion volunteers to take out a German gun picking off Canadian soldiers." Pete was first to raise his hand. His platoon was held up by uncut wire; alone he dashed through an opening on the flank, rushing the machine gun. after a life-or-death struggle with its crew he captured the gun then trained it on its former   proprietors. His gallantry enabled the platoon to advance, said the 8 Jan 1918 London Gazette. Two of his battalion's snipers were wounded & exposed in German counter-attacks. Robertson ventured into danger & brought one back safely. Enemy fighters trained their sights on him then. As he went back for the second soldier, he was hit under heavy fire. He fell, staggered back up, lifted the injured sniper to his shoulder & returned towards the Canadian line. Slipping & stumbling, he lay the man down to safety. A shell exploded nearby, killing Robertson. "They said he was a humble type of person, that he wouldn't have seen it as bravery — just what needed to be done," said his great-niece Lynne Rockwell Tebay. PHOTOS: courtesy Lynne Rockwell Tebay

CANADA AVENUE

Horrific numbers/
Canada's 100 Days
A hundred days in late 1917
Almost half a million die to gain 8km
Four men killed for every metre of that road
The final 900 metres
took 2,238 casualties
where Mother Canada
wept maple leaves & poppies
Less than a kilometre from farm to church
on the village square
Marked by Canadian granite in one massive block
Almost as hard as war itself/
    Almost as hard as the sacrifice
    of men plunged into a rain-clogged quagmire/
    gunned down & shelled
    1st World War
    2nd Battle of Passchendaele
    3rd Battle of Ypres
    {Forth they went}[32]

PHOTO by J. Carmichael/The view from farm to church square down Canada Avenue at Passchendaele

---

[32] "And finally in 1917 the Ypres sector came to the climax of its story in that tragedy of blood, mud and futility, the Passchendaele offensive." - Charles Henry Savage of Eastman, Quebec, 5th Canadian Mounted Rifles

In the Second Battle of Passchendaele, between 26 October - 10 November 1917
4,000 Canadian lads died; another 12,000 were wounded. That last critical stretch of road has been renamed Canada Avenue. Victoria crosses were awarded to:
acting Capt. Christopher O'Kelly of the 52nd (Ontario) Battalion
Sgt. Robert Shankland of the 43rd (Cameron Highlanders) Battalion
Pte. Thomas William Holmes of the 4th Canadian Mounted Rifles Battalion
Pte. Cecil John Kinross of the 49th (Edmonton) Battalion
Sgt. George Mullin of the Princess Patricia's Canadian Light Infantry
acting Maj. George Pearkes of the 5th Canadian Mounted Rifles Battalion
Lt. Hugh McKenzie of the 7th Canadian Machine Gun Company*
Cpl. Colin Fraser Barron of the 3rd (Toronto) Battalion
Pte. James Peter Robertson of the 27th (City of Winnipeg) Battalion*
    *deceased in battle

MMP17/ZONNEBEKE/BELGIUM

Crosses grazing like sheep
flock the countryside
dotted with graveyards
on hills/pastoral now
Besides memorials & gravestones
scattered over hillocks left
by trenches & craters – besides those/
few signs of the chaos of
a century ago remain
The restored grand farmhouse
The Passchendaele Museum

Try on a Commonwealth helmet
Feel the weight of it on your head
Hoist unwieldy protective armour
{No Kevlar for those warriors}
Sniff harmless versions of lethal gases
Feel & smell war

Step down/way down/big step
underground dugouts
600 metres of trenches/
carved out cave-like tunnels/like shafts
Mossy signs of life midst
decay on ancient sandbags
It's eerie/walking where war was mined
Imagine another generation
living under here/
#Could you do it?

MMP17 HAIKU

So many young men
clambered into the trenches
Fewer clambered out

PHOTO J. Carmichael/An exhibit at MMP17 Museum (Passchendaele)/Zonnebeke

SOMEWHERE IN FRANCE 25 DEC 1917

"... We had chicken for dinner
and also the allowance of Plum Pudding, which was very good.
The chicken could have been younger.
There was snow about 2" when we came here
but it disappeared last night
and tonight it is snowing heavy again...
One thing this place is full of rats
and some of them are larger than most cats or at least look it.
The Battery was here a considerable time
before they made their last move
so the place is like home to all except the new men.
... It seems hard to be throwing shells at one another on Xmas Day
but I suppose they cannot stop the war even for the day
Wood is more plentiful here and we can get all we want
out of the ruins of houses just outside our door
Any buildings that still stand
have their walls punctured with shell holes"
- *Robert Shortreed*

Excerpts from a letter from Robert Shortreed of Guelph, Ontario to his sister,
and photo (he is left, on the second row) courtesy CanadianLetters.ca / VIU

#1918

**Other Canadian WWI Theatres
opening up include:**
North-West Persia & Caspian
1918-1919
Murmansk 1918-1919
Archangel 1918-1919
Siberia 1918-1919
March-June 1918:
The German Offensives 1918
– First Battles of the Somme 1918,
St. Quentin, Actions at Somme
Crossings, First Bapaume, Rosieres,
First Arras 1918, Avre, Capture of Hamel,
the Lys, Estaires (First Defence of Givenchy),
Hazebrouck, Messines 1918 (Loss of Hill 63),
First Kemmel Ridge, Action of La Becque
8-11 Aug. 1918:
Battle of Amiens, spearheaded by
Canadian Corps, 9,074 Canadian casualties.
8 Aug to 11 Nov 1918:
The Hundred Days. Advance to Victory/Germans 'Retreat to Mons'
– Damery, Scarpe, Second Battles of the Somme 1918, Albert 1918, Second Bapaume,
Second Battles of Arras 1918, Scarpe 1918 (Monchy-le-Preuz),
Drocourt-Queant Canal, Battles of the Hindenburg Line, Havrincourt, Epehy,
Canal de Nord (Capture of Bourlon Wood), St Quentin Canal, Beaurevoir Line,
Cambrai 1918, Pursuit to the Selle, Courtrai, the Selle, Valenciennes
(capture of Moot Hill), the Sambre, Passage of the Grande Honnelle, Capture of Mons.

11 November 1918:
Armistice stops the shooting/shelling at 11:11 a.m. /
9 million service personnel, 20 million civilians killed in war/
With millions of prisoners of war on both sides, complete extrication will take a lot longer

PHOTO by Richard Houghton: stained glass at Kettlewell Church in Britain, honouring the North Yorkshire vicar's son Sgt John Cockerill, killed in action at Bailleul.

THE WAR'S TOP SNIPER

Not a wing nor breath stirs
in the small hours
of No Man's Land/
but silent feet trace a path

Patient & still
as the hunting owl
in the starless night/
waiting long/aiming true[33]

PHOTO by J. Carmichael: Portrait of Lance Cpl. Francis Pegahmagabow at Memorial Museum Passchendaele (MMP17)

---

[33] Acting Lance Cpl. Francis Pegahmagabow of the Anishinaabe and the Shawanaga First Nation was the most successful sniper of WWI. His Ross rifle stopped a record 378 enemy soldiers. He captured 300 enemy soldiers. He overcame discriminatory practices 'exempting' First Nations from the 'eligibility' to enlist, signing up in the first wave of Canadians to volunteer in August 1914. He was one of the first Canadians of WWI to be awarded the Military Medal. His commendation reads: "He carried messages with great bravery and success during the whole of the actions at Ypres, Festubert and Givenchy. In all his work he has consistently shown a disregard for danger and his faithfulness to duty is highly commendable." At Passchendaele in 1917, he earned his first bar to the MM. His commendation reads: "At Passchendaele Nov. 6th/7th, 1917, this NCO [non-commissioned officer] did excellent work. Before and after the attack he kept in touch with the flanks, advising the units he had seen, this information proving the success of the attack and saving valuable time in consolidating. He also guided the relief to its proper place after it had become mixed up." Wounds at the Somme couldn't stop him; he earned a rare second bar to the Military Medal at the Battle of the Scarpe in August 1918 at Orix Trench, going over the top under heavy fire to bring back ammunition to assist in repulsing heavy enemy counter-attacks. One of only 39 Canadians to earn a second bar to the Military Medal, after the war he served the Wasauksing First Nation as chief, leader and organizer. He was outspoken for indigenous rights and self-determination. A bronze statue at Parry Sound shows Pegahmagabow with his Ross rifle, a caribou beside him and an eagle on his arm.

IN THE BOOK

From the book "Mrs. Private Peat" (1918)
by Louisa "Bebe" Watson Small Peat /
Irish-born author & lecturer,
Black Jack's correspondent
writes about him.

168   MRS. PRIVATE PEAT

friend George A. Vowel. Corporal Vowel is known among his comrades as "Black Jack." He is a native American, from Texas, was holding down a homestead at Hanna, Alberta, when war broke out and he there and then enlisted with the famous Tenth.

Jack was a machine gunner and distinguished himself early in 1917 when he held back, manning his gun single-handed, an attack of a German company. For this Jack was awarded the Military Medal. He is the only soldier I know who has been in the scrap since August of 1914 and who has not been wounded, although he has been in every fight with the Tenth and later with the Thirteenth Battalion. But he has been in hospital twice—once with mumps and once with measles.

It was Jack who in one of his letters, spoke of a reunion which was held by all who remained of the original Tenth. This was in April of '16. There were then thirty-two of the men alive in France. To-day, if there are three others besides Jack, I am surprised.

Jack came to see us on his leave of 1915. It was in November and he and young Art Chis-

BLACK JACK/LOUISA 'BEBE' WATSON SMALL PEAT

He never knew   a woman like*
his lovely wartime pen-pal   Louisa 'Bebe' Watson Peat /*
He may have been secretly crazy for her / She married a bonafide hero*
With brilliant prospects / Private Harry Peat of Edmonton who fought*
underweight to get into the CEF by "faking" a few pounds / / / In battle he *
lost the use of his arm / became the perfect recruiter /Gifted writer Louisa*
Watson Peat would keep his letters / CBC made a radio program of them*
decades after he was gone /& her daughter gave copies to Peggy Vowel*
Aston who then gave them to her niece/Bebe mapped some trails *
through war history with her book 'Mrs. Private Peat' paving*
them with letters from soldiers/turned into clean*
white pages // read between the tidy lines*
for fascinating   stories about*
fellows like Black*
Jack*

Louise
"Bebe"
Watson
Small
Peat

170   MRS. PRIVATE PEAT

was all against us—our boys who stood in water and mud and blood for weeks on end because there were no others to relieve them—our boys who died—who passed on long since. Only the glory of memory is theirs—I would plead with you of the Allies, new and old—do not forget them. It was they who saved you. The boys to-day, no less brave, yet are but *completing* a victory already begun.

Jack Vowel's letters are in themselves an epitome of the war. He has a power of description, a sense of contrast and a sense of humor, rarely combined. For such as he—and for the brave boys who are going daily now, there is not much that we can do—a prayer, a thought, a cheery note, a small something to show that they are not forgotten—that we are grateful.

JUST CALL HIM ANGEL OF THE TRENCHES

At 2, immigrated with his family from the Azores to America /
Another Hispanic immigrant kid/in search of a better life
A brilliant student/fluent in six languages
For Fr. Joao (John) Baptista DeValles/a better life meant service
Priest/pastor/parochial school founder
Enlisted as a U.S. Army Chaplain with the104th Reg. of 26th Inf. "Yankee Division"
A soft touch/he made "loans" to the men/
writing it in his journal/then ripping out the notes/
Nicknamed "Angel of the Trenches"
10-13 April 1918 he put himself repeatedly in harm's way at Apremont /
braving heavy artillery & machine guns to bring the wounded to safety

When his hands were too numb to carry stretchers
he looped telephone wire to his wrists
to hold them

11 March 1918/rendered gallant service
at Chemin des Dames/
staying with the wounded
during heavy bombardment
One night they found him wounded/
at the side of a dead soldier
he had ministered to
He was given the French Croix de Guerre
for "extraordinary heroism and exceptional
devotion to duty, under uninterrupted fire and
the constant risk of his life" {awddistrict.org}
& the French Legion of Honour
No time to rest on his laurels
Fr. DeValles died in 1920 from
complication of wounds in battle
& mustard gas

They pinned the U.S. Army's
Distinguished Service Cross
on his chest
in the casket
According to the Catholic Stand
all New Bedford mourned
RIP Angel of the Trenches

SIDE BY SIDE

Not so different
The two of them/
{on the German side}
Brothers in arms
in World War I
at the Second Battle
of the Somme
Doing what their
country asked of them
Not so different
Dying within
a few days
of each other
Buried side by side
Two decades
away from
another war
another kind of chaos
Then it will be different

PHOTO by Daphne Vangheluwe: German soldiers Lt. Julius Bauer, (one of 9 German soldiers with a Jewish gravestone at Rancourt Deutscher Soldat Friedhof out of 11,422) and musketeer August Buhler, with a Christian gravestone. Both died in March, 1918. Restorations/new stones started in 1972. At the cemetery, there are two mass graves of 7,492 soldiers, only 2,316 of whom are known by name

1st AMERICAN AWARDED CROIX DE GUERRE WITH STAR & BRONZED PALM

Sgt. William Henry Johnson/American soldier/Uncommonly courageous
Like his fellow African-Americans/discriminated against in American ranks
but accepted quite happily/fully by the French

In the Argonne Forest/14 May 1918
during hand-to-hand combat/suffering from 21 wounds
the Albany New York resident fought off the enemy
with grenades/rifle butt/Bolo knife & bare fists/all he had
rescuing another soldier
He returned to the States but honours would come along
long after he was gone
The Purple Heart
     {67 years after his death}
The Distinguished Service Cross
     {73 years after his death}
The Medal of Honor
     {86 years after his death}
Better late than never/Earlier would have been better
Honour his valour always/RIP Sgt. Henry Johnson

PHOTO Library of Congress: Sgt. William Henry Johnson, the first American ever awarded France's Croix de Guerre with Star & Bronzed Palm. For Johnson, the worst fight though/was against prejudice vicious & rampant/was still to come/at home in America where he gave speeches/found interest/admiration until jealousy/discrimination reared its head. He died destitute in 1929 from untreated tuberculosis.

KINDNESS BLOOMS/NEAR/FAR

Kindness blooms near
Near the end of the war she was
Near the front lines to be
Near the wounded which put her
Near the battle & so very
Near to danger looming near
Nursing Sister
Gladys Maud Mary Wake
34 / So far away from
the Class of 1912 at
Royal Jubilee nursing school
& her native Esquimalt, B.C.

Nursing Sister Gladys Mary Maud Wake rests
near where she died
May 21, 1918 of air raid wounds
Near the 1st Canadian General Hospital/
Etaples/Pas de Calais/France
Far from home
Near other women who died in the same raid
Near to the lads who called her Sister
Near to the heart of those who remember
Kindness flowers where it's needed most
Near the front lines /
where the targets are
Like white lilies in
fields of red poppies
Kindness blooms
& when temporal things fade
& time slips far away
with distant memories
The kindness remains near

PHOTOS: Gladys Maud Mary Wake Images Veterans.gc.ca from a newspaper clipping; poppies from Pixabay

DAMN THE TORPEDOES/HOSPITAL SHIP LLANDOVERY CASTLE

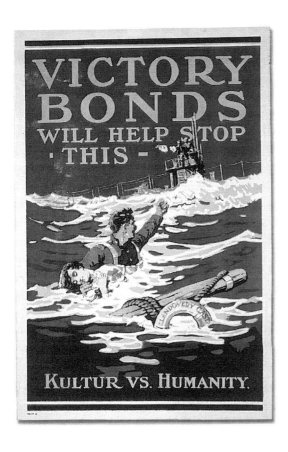

SOS /SOS
WWI torpedoes
No respecters of
persons/ Of class
or gender / or of
non - combatants
those who goDown
to the sea in ships/
27 June 1918/SOS
/The Hospital Ship
// Llandovery//
Castle // CNMS
/the Canadian/
Naval Medical
Service//After
delivering ill/
Canadians /
home/sunk in
10 minutes
byGerman
sub U-86
of 258
all 14 nursing
sisters aboard die
just 24   survive

`   Killed include Canadian Army Medical Corps'
Margaret Marjorie Fraser, daughter of the Lieutenant Governor of British Columbia
& Rena Maud McLean, daughter of Senator John McLean of PEI /
Lost to a watery grave /Savagery for those in peril on the sea/
Escaping lifeboats are deliberately sunk/
SOS[34]

34 According to warmuseum.ca, 2,504 Canadian nurses served overseas in World War I. They were nicknamed "bluebirds" because of their uniforms. POSTER courtesy Government of Ontario Archive.

INDRA LAL "LADDIE" ROY

He'll go for the skies
The wide open air
& a plane to make his mark
Time for Oxford later
Forever 19
He'll go for the skies

A native of Calcutta, Indra Lal "Laddie" Roy was a London schoolboy when war broke out. A gifted student whose design for a better trench mortar received notice and helped earn him an Oxford scholarship, he was keen to fly and sought to join the Royal Flying Corps. He sold his motorbike to pay for a second opinion on his eyesight after being excluded as unfit to fly. He won his place in the clouds and a post with the RFC's No. 56 Squadron, flying SE5 Scouts, quickly earning victories and a reputation as an "ace." On 22 July 1918, he was shot down over German territory by four enemy Fokker DVIIs. According to blogger Sanchari Pal at TheBetterIndia.com, the Red Baron {Manfred von Richtofen} paid his respects & sent flowers – a wreath dropped where Roy's plane had crashed. Roy was posthumously given the Distinguished Flying Cross. He is buried at Estevelles/100km north of the grave of another Indian combat pilot of the era, Lt. Srikrishna Wellingkar. Indra Lal Roy's nephew, Subroto Mukerjee, would serve as a fighter pilot in WWII and become the first Chief of Air Staff of the Indian Air Force. Roy was honoured with an Indian stamp on the 100th anniversary of his birth. TOP PHOTO/public domain/ bottom photo TSRL "The Shuttleworth Trust's SE5A at Old Warden's Summer Show 2009"

RED CROSS FARM

"A symbol of French-American friendship
A call for peace among nations"
The 42nd Rainbow Division
Croix Rouge Farm
at Fère-en-Tardenois
where 162 soldiers
from Alabama
& their Iowa comrades died

A bronze soldier carries the body
of his dead comrade
Forever the witness of the sacrifice
of young Americans July 26, 1918[35]

PHOTO by Fotoshoot WO1oo (Nick Mol) The 42nd Rainbow Division Memorial at Croix Rouge Farm at Fère-en-Tardenois France

---

[35] Text from the memorial, unveiled in 2011. According website, croixrougefarm.org, the memorial artist, James Butler, says he was "in the army myself and have a great admiration and sympathy for the lot of the common soldier and how sometimes the most ordinary man will rise to the heights of great bravery and concern for his fellow soldier. In the 42nd Rainbow Division memorial, my original idea was to portray the powerful bond between men on active service with a soldier carrying his dead comrade. However after working on the sculpture for some time the piece began to have a strong spiritual meaning for me. The dead soldier is limp as if his body had just been lifted from the battlefield. The figure holding the dead man began to have the presence of the Angel of Mercy. He is perfect – there are no battle scars on him and he is untouched by the grim conflict. I am not a religious man, but working on this sculpture I felt a strong spiritual guidance."

BLACK JACK/PURSUIT TO MONS

Like to punch his lights out
That lad in my dress picture
he sure looks cocky/
eager to step up/
'do his bit'
I'd like to go back there/
somehow elude the laws of the universe
Transport myself to travel back in time
Shake up his patriotic self/
talk sense into him/
punch his lights out if I had to
Nobody made him go/
He put his hand up
He volunteered soon as he could
/I'd take it back if I could
Immersed in war's grim realities
from the first major action
by the First Canadian Division
to the war's last gasps as
the enemy retreats/*Field of dead Germans*
uniformed bodies ready to be harvested
10 August 1918/Beauchamp le Benix
We camp on ground taken from Fritz
the boys must have went through them like a whirlwind
Must try to remember why I am here/I am done/I am played out
I look like a loose button on an overcoat/
I am the 15th Alberta Light Horse/
I am the 10th Battalion CEF

BLACK JACK/DESOLATION

Country blazing fire
Both sides seeing just how much
ammo they can waste

PHOTO: George 'Black Jack' Vowel, thin as a rail mid-war, seated, with another soldier
/courtesy Brian Vowel

AN IMAGINED LETTER TO DANIEL & CATHERINE ALTY

Dear Mr & Mrs Alty
Our condolences on the loss of your two sons
Your oldest, Pte. Thomas Alty, 32,
a gunner with the Tank Corps
KIA 23 Nov 1917 at Cambrai.
Your middle son, 2nd Lt. Daniel, 31,
with 2nd Battalion South Staffordshire Regiment,
died 5 Sep 1918/buried at Anneaux
We will grant your application
for home service
for your remaining son, Henry, 24,
your youngest,
since you've already lost two sons
Congratulations, by the way,
on his Distinguished Conduct Medal
Henry is loath to leave
his fellows in arms
Again, we honour your sacrifice,
and we will send him
back to Westhead
Sincerely,
Your Country

Dear Mr & Mrs Alty,
Please accept our condolences
on the loss of
your third and youngest son, Henry,
killed in action 30 Sep 1918,
the same day
your application for home service
was granted
The tragic irony of this
supreme sacrifice
does not go unobserved.
We remain,
Your Country

PHOTOS public domain / courtesy St James Church/Westhead

THE INCREDIBLE TRUE STORY OF CHER AMI & HIS MEDALS

```
                    \
                    c\                                    cher ami
        \           c\\\\                                 our dear friend
    C\\             c\\\\\                    3Of great valour/
      C\ you        c\\\\\\\\\      _____ flying fast /flying hurt\\\\
        C\\ carry the message for the Lost Battalion/U.S. 77th Infantry Division
        C \\ trapped behind enemy lines/without food or ammunition/cut off
          C \\ in a pocket of woods/weak & dwindling/sure to perish under
          C\\ enemy/friendly fire 3 Oct 1918  in the Argonne Forest/tiny
            C \\ critical message strapped to your leg : "Our artillery is
            C\\ dropping a barrage  directly on  us . For  heaven's
              C\\ sake,  stop! Whittlesay, Maj. 308th" You are
                      / wounded  by  shrapnel,  shot  through  the
                      /breast,  one  leg shot  almost off / blinded
                      / in one eye /  still   you arrive  at your loft
                      / just 25 minutes later in bloody triumph
                      /& your determination saves 194 men
                       / Medics scramble to save you
                     /When you leave France for === \\\
                    /Well-earned rest                    \\\
                  / /General Pershing\\                   \\\
                /sees you off  / //You earn the        //. //
              / Croix  de Guerre / Palm with Oak Cluster    \  /. \/. \/.
          \When you die in 1919 you are stuffed / Your final loft
          U/The Smithsonian Museum/Our fine-feathered friend\
            U  U. U. U. U. U. U. U. U. U. U. U. U. U. U\\\_
```

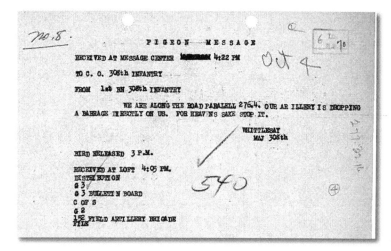

Cher Ami (French for "dear friend) was one of 600 pigeons trained for the U.S. Army Signal Corps in France in World War I. {The system was aided with the invention of the motorized portable dovecote, basically a motorhome for carrier pigeons.} When Charles Whittlesay and his men became trapped behind enemy lines without food or ammunition, pigeons bearing the messages "Many wounded. We cannot evacuate" and "Men are suffering. Can support be sent?" were shot down, but the last pigeon, Cher Ami, survived to wing the critical message home.

GOOD DOG, SGT. STUBBY!

Sgt. Stubby went to Yale
That is where we start our tail
A loveable stray who found a friend
to stick with to the very end
Robert Conroy took the terrier to war
He thought, "Comradeship, a dog is for!"
Stubby soon learned that war is ruff
But to be with the troops, for him, was enough
Stubby heard first enemy artillery whine
He'd bark "Incoming!" on the front line
He'd venture to No Man's Land to find men in need
Returning, wag his tail to say, "Lads, follow my lead!"
Wounded by a grenade at Chemin des Dames
They gave him first aid so he wouldn't succumb
He was sent to the rear to convalesce
& brighten morale – Stubby couldn't do less
After being gassed he was given his own mask
& he learned to detect gas, and other tasks
He really proved himself in France
He caught an enemy soldier by the seat of the pants!
Grateful women of Chateau-Thierry sewed a coat for his medals
– tres haute mode!
After the war he went to Georgetown Law
With that tail/those big eyes, the attention he'd draw...
After the U.S. 102nd Infantry Regiment/
Stubby met three American presidents
He lives on a century later at the Smithsonian Museum
If you visit him there
it certainly would please him

At ease Sgt Stubby/Good dog! [36]

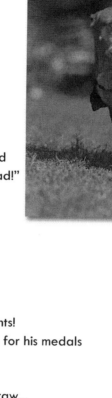

---

[36] PHOTOS public domain. Stubby was a regiment mascot. Other furry enlisters, Red Cross dogs were picked for their smarts - keen of nose/sharp in vision. Thousands trained to ignore heavy fire, to venture despite terror out into No Man's Land, to wear a gas mask/to distinguish between the living & the dead, to recognize a Commonwealth uniform/to bring medicine & water, to return with evidence & summon help if the injured man is unable to move. One of the most famous was an Airdale terrier named Jack who/despite mortal wounds/ delivered a critical message to save a unit. Brave dog.

ON THE ARGONNE BATTLE

God would never be cruel enough to create a cyclone as terrible as that Argonne battle. Only man would ever think of doing an awful thing like that. It looked like "the abomination of desolation" must look like.
And all through the long night those big guns flashed and growled just like the lightning and the thunder when it storms in the mountains at home.
And, oh my, we had to pass the wounded. And some of them were on stretchers going back to the dressing stations, and some of them were lying around, moaning and twitching. And the dead were all along the road. And it was wet and cold. And it all made me think of the Bible and the story of the Anti-Christ and Armageddon.
And I'm telling you the little log cabin in Wolf Valley in old Tennessee seemed a long long way off."   — *Sgt. (Cpl.) Alvin C. York* [37]

PHOTO/Sgt. (Cpl.) Alvin Cullum York/public domain

---

[37] Caught by the enemy in the cove of a hill in the Forest of Argonne, 8 Oct 1918, he did not run; but sank into the bushes and single-handed fought a battalion of German machine gunners until he made them come down that hill to him with their hands in air. There were one hundred and thirty-two of them left, and he marched them, prisoners, into the American line. Marshal Foch, in decorating him, said, "What you did was the greatest thing accomplished by any private soldier of all of the armies of Europe." — Sam K. Cowan, author of *Sergeant York & His People*. Sgt. (Cpl.) Alvin Cullum York, earned the American Medal of Honour for capturing a German machine gun nest. The attack yielded 32 machine guns, 28 enemy soldiers dead and 132 enemy soldiers taken POW. A biopic with Gary Cooper was a hit years later.

CONSPICUOUS BRAVERY & DEVOTION TO DUTY

In St John's, Newfoundland
a memorial recalls a pharmacy/
a pharmacist/Thomas Ricketts
As a fisherman/as a boy/
he quietly added 3 years to his age to enlist with the Royal Newfoundland
Regiment
On 14 Oct. 1918, Pte. Ricketts volunteered
to brave heavy battery fire to advance
with the Lewis gun and his section commander/
They ran out of ammunition under heavy fire
Pte. Ricketts' "presence of mind in anticipating the enemy intention & his utter disregard of personal
safety" {not to mention his willingness to dash through heavy machine gun fire to fetch more
ammo}/saved the day
But for Pte. Ricketts saying he was 18 when he was 15,
the native of Middle Arm, White Bay
never would have been admitted to the RNR
He'd never have been wounded at Cambrai & recovered in England
& never become the youngest recipient of the Victoria Cross
for Conspicuous Bravery & Devotion to Duty,

{& the Croix de Guerre avec Etoile
d'Or}
before returning home
to go to school
to become a pharmacist at the
corner of Job & Water Streets
The pharmacy's gone but
the memorial remains
to Pte. Ricketts & to Conspicuous
Bravery & Devotion to Duty

PHOTOS by Lies Depuydt: public event at Thomas Ricketts Memorial at
Sint-Eloois Winkel in Belgium.

PROMISES TO KEEP

Give women the vote! Bring in Prohibition!
Away with Political Corruption & Patronage in Civil Service!
Improve Workmen's Comp! Better Labour Laws!
Campaign promises of BC Premier Harlan Carey Brewster
Cannery operator/Leader of the Opposition
MLA for Port Alberni/MLA for Victoria

No class exemption
from war nor from
heartbreak
BC Premier Harlan
Brewster in office long
enough to keep
the first two promises
He died unexpectedly
1 March 1918
{mercifully perhaps}
He did not live to hear
news his son/
gunner Ray Brewster
was killed instantly
1 Nov 1918 when the gun
he was operating
received a direct hit
just 10 days
before Armistice

Ray Harlan Brewster and fellow soldiers
PHOTO: courtesy from the Harold Monks collection CanadianLetters.ca / VIU

PERSISTENCE - WALTER T. ROBUS

I received a bomb in the face {24 July 1915} it did not explode but cracked the jaw bone & cut my mouth, & broke my teeth up on one side ... rather painful, still I must not grumble ... If I had not have moved as I did I should have got it in the head & would have probably been killed but it was not to be & so therefore I am spared. After about 6 weeks I elected to be sent back to the line & here I am nearly as fit as ever & ready to do a little more to help crush the Bosche

15 Feb 1916: "... At first thought I would lose my right leg, but they have fixed it up pretty good; Two of the pieces made lovely holes right through the thigh, one about the size of a 25-cent piece & the other bigger, fairly let the daylight into me

March 17, 1916: "... Three months electrical treatment for my legs, but I am trying to get out at the end of the month & rejoin the Battalion in France; I still walk with a limp but can consider myself very lucky to get off with that

15 May 1916: " I had a Board & was told I was permanently unfit, but I managed to come away with a little persuasion; Think I have done my bit already, but something made me come again, don't know why ...

14 June 1916: "I got a shrapnel bullet-clean through shoulder & my badge saved it from going through my neck, so I am once more on my back for a week or two, still I am doing fine & hope to have another crack at Fritz in the future

19 Sept 1916: "... Was marked unfit for further Active Service, but when I feel a bit stronger I shall try again for the front, as I like it better than these hospitals; Enclosed is a small trench snap taken at Messines, showing myself in shirt sleeves, all the others in the picture are killed

24 Nov 1916: "... Asked to be given another trip to France, but they just laughed at me & told me they wanted fit men, so I guess I have to take a back seat; Am trying very hard to get a chance in one of the tanks, may strike it lucky

PHOTO: WWI Victory Medal given to George "Black Jack" Anderson Vowel, one of 351,289 issued to CEF. A total of 5,725,000 were issued.

8 Jan 1917: "... Did you notice one of my bombers (Lou Clarke of Winnipeg.) gained the V.C. & several have D.C.Ms. & military medals, so far I have not had the luck, so would like another turn

12 Feb 1917: "They want me to do clerical work in London, but I have thought the whole matter over seriously, & have decided to carry on for while till I get a little stronger physically ... I think I will take another chance, in fact something seems to call me back again, I have had that same feeling each & every time I have been back to France, & somehow I think a fellow when he feels that way, he ought to go; Mind you, nobody wants to be shot at, have had quite sufficient, but we old boys, took the oath when we 'listed & we have a lot of debts to pay, so those of us that are left must & will finish what our comrades who have fallen cannot do; They have given their all, their life's blood, & we have to fight on

17 June 1918: "...I have managed after a struggle to get back again to France & hope to be able to present Fritz with a few souvenirs soon ... there is no danger as to the ultimate ending to this show; Personally I feel just as optimistic now as when I first came across, & in fact a little more so

18 Nov. 1918: "The Peace celebrations here have been immense, everybody frantic with joy & excitement; What a relief to the parents of the boys serving!! & what a relief to know the slaughter & suffering are over; Willie (Kaiser Wilhelm of Germany) should be treated as he deserves & not allowed to get away light; The soldiers should have the handling of him ... The Canadians finished wonderful"[38]

PHOTO: Practice bull's-eye of Douglas G. Buckley, Guysborough, NS / CanadianLetters.ca

---

[38] Excerpts from letters from Walter Thomas Robus of Norwood, Ontario to Rev. A.M. Irwin. Robus was the first man in town to sign up for the war, joining the "Suicide Club" – the First Canadian Contingent bomb squad. He saw the Second Battle of Ypres and The Somme, spending a fair amount of time crawling close to the German lines armed with a pistol and pockets full of bombs. His bouts with wounds are confirmed in Robus' government medical records, which also cite bouts of tonsillitis and influenza. Several mentions in his records that he is "dangerously ill." He survived the war but died young in 1926, and his employer put up a bronze memorial plaque in honour of his war service. Letters courtesy CanadianLetters.ca

TICKLED TO DEATH/GEORGE WALTER ADAMS

Following wire received at about 0730 hours this am: "Hostilities will cease at 1100hours 11/11/18 AAA Troops will stand fast on line reached at that hour which will be reported by wire to Army HQ as soon as possible AAA Defence precautions will be maintained AAA There will be no intercourse with enemy until receipt of instructions from GHQ AAA Further instructions follow AAA". Needless to say we are all tickled to death and there's been all sort of celebrations during the day. Whale of a blow out in the officers mess last night. The next question is when will we get home."

— Journal entry from George Walter Adams

WOULD YOU LIKE TO BURN THE KAISER?/EMILY ADAMS

George's mother Emily Adams wrote this about Armistice Day 11 Nov 1918 to him in a letter:

I wished you were home last Monday as I think you would have enjoyed the fun. At 4.30am Edie carne into my room & said "Can't you hear the racket. The Armistice is signed." I made her go back to bed & to make sure she did I got into her bed & she chatted away & wondered if anyone would come over. I said "not at this time of the morning" but sure enough a few minutes after Nellie, Eva, Zeta, Annie & Dorothy carne with saucepan lids & old tin cans. They made a dreadful noise; took Edie out; called for Lil; then went parading the streets till breakfast time. I expect Edie will write & tell you all about what they did downtown. About 11 o'clock Mrs. Campbell carne over & asked me to go up there but I didn't go until the evening. Hadn't been in long when Mr. Wykes sent in to say he was going to burn the Kaiser, would we like to join in the fun. So we all went out & there was a huge bonfire in front of their house & when that. died down a bit Mr. McCaw brought out a lot of boxes which made it scorching hot."

Life went on, but it was different. By a Dec. 18 letter, Emily had news had come that a family friend, Dan, was "shell-shocked" and unable to come straight home or see his family. By Dec. 26, there was more news: "Tuesday morn Eva came over to tell me she had just received a few lines from Dan. He said he was very ill & couldn't write any better. We were all so relieved to think he was able to do that much."

An immigrant from England, George Walter Adams enlisted as a clerk in October 1916 in Toronto and returned after the war. Four years earlier, on 16 Nov 1918 his journal read: "16 Nov 1914
All city regiments notified to be at armories at 2.30 this afternoon. As soon as notified the men had to rush home from their employment, don their uniforms and hustle to the armouries. The sight of men lacing their boots and putting on their uniforms on the street cars caused much alarm among the general public and rumour had it that the Germans were on their way from Detroit to invade Canada." Journal excerpts courtesy CanadianLetters.ca

"TANKED" CANADA'S GERMAN PRISONERS FOLLOW THE TANK.

18 NOV 1918 / DEAREST PAL

I have just finished your Peace letter of the 11th/Like you I can hardly believe it is true/though we are all beginning to settle down to the idea/It seems too marvellous that it is all over at last & that I shall have my darling at home with me again/The {German?} helmet came all safe & is such a beauty - the men were all so interested in it & I have promised to photograph most of them with it on

I have just come home from the Coliseum/I took five of the men & when we got out in the street to come home/there was such a jam I didn't know how I should even navigate them along/Buses were out of the question & so we decided to try the Tube ...We came out at Charing Cross ... so jammed I was almost in despair when I saw a taxi unloading just beside me

I rushed up & told the taxi man I had five blind soldiers & must get home

... We all filed in & drove home in comfort & I was so pleased & relieved

that I gave him ten shillings/He nearly fell off his perch but I felt it was worth it/

Besides it is Peace Week!

You must feel at rather a loose end having nothing to do after all the excitement

The last week, dearie, has been the hardest I have had for I was so afraid

something might happen at the very last/I went down on my knees, dearie,

when I knew for sure you were coming back to me

All love & kisses from your little pal, Alice Leighton[39]

PHOTO: Canada's German prisoners follow the tank/courtesy CanadianLetters.ca / VIU

---

[39] Arthur Leighton lived in Manitoba before fighting in the Boer War and then attending law school at the University of Manitoba. He married Alice Wright & practiced law in Nanaimo, B.C. before enlisting. Alice followed him, working as a VAD in England. Postwar, the Leightons returned to Nanaimo.

Servicemen (including Robert Shortreed) on leave mark Armistice 11 Nov 1918 with a photo during a visit to Versailles, France (CanadianLetters.ca)

BRITISH ARMY & NAVY LEAVE/CLUB /VERSAILLES FRANCE/12 NOV 1918

My Dear Mother:
... You will have heard the good news that the Armistice has been signed
which is at least the beginning of the end if not the end
Anyway it is being celebrated as the end here
Yesterday Paris was crazy with joy and streets were impassable for people
Today is going to be almost as bad/Flags are to be seen everywhere
The French way of showing their joy is to kiss everyone
and few people escaped it yesterday
Of course the soldiers came in for their share
Parades were innumerable and I was in one of British soldiers
headed by the Horse Guards Band but it was impossible to get through the crowd and the Band did
not have a chance to walk let alone play
It was simply a mob all day long ...
Have sent you on a book of postcards and also
a photo we had taken on Saturday on a trip to the Palace at Versailles
where the Peace Conference is expected to be held ... Love to all, Rob

#1919&1920

28 June 1919:
After six months of Allied negotiations at the Paris Peace Conference & occupying Germany, Canada signs Treaty of Versailles — five years to the day after Archduke Franz Ferdinand's assassination; Article 231, the "War Guild Clause" requires Germany to disarm & make the equivalent of over $440 billion (2018 U.S. dollars) of reparations.

The arrangements please hardly anybody at the table.

PHOTOS: Koln (Cologne) Cathedral postcard, CanadianLetters.ca;
Chicago welcomes home the 370th Regiment {Old 8th Illinois}
Public domain/courtesy BlackHistoryHeroes.com

O LITTLE TOWN OF ARKHOLME!

How blest with returning sons you are
Arthur Mee noted the rarity & named you a Thankful Village
You sent 59 of your best sons {fathers, brothers, sweethearts}
to face the War Monster & every last man – all 59 – returned home
Safe but not necessarily unchanged
Escaping the law of An Eye For An Eye
Think of it! Happy consequences

Bucking probabilities: All who go/come back!
Above thy deep & dreamless sleep
the entire war goes by/
Twilight Zone unbreakable
Insurance bean-counters
mightn't've predicted it
How silently, how silently
this wondrous gift is giv'n
The hopes & fears of all the war years
as mothers & fathers & sweethearts
held their collective lucky breath
did they pray/drum fingers?
did they cultivate ulcers & twitches?
Bookmakers might pause at the odds
at a handful of towns with this phenomenon
A cynic might say "Buy a lottery ticket!"/
wonder about rates & dates
of volunteerism vs. conscription
Yet in thy blackout-dark streets shineth
no need for survivor guilt
considering all everyone was subjected to/
like the rest of us whose grandfathers returned/

Home but not unscathed/different for all they had seen
We too are Thankful Villages/those of us who had one veteran at a time
Returning to brighten their family's doorways/but not untouched/still different
Tears are due for those whose losses were more bitter/but
We rejoice with you on the blissful statistical anomaly
that shaped your town's DNA
{& wonder if your communal lucky streak continued
& if it was something in the water}

PHOTO: courtesy Pixabay

BLACK JACK/NOT A BUCKET LIST

Opposite of a bucket list/
the list of things
that happened to me
Like the list of things you'd
never want to happen to you/ever
Delivering rations to the front/
dodging bullets & mortar fire both
Bullets ripped the dirt up all round me but
none of them were marked Black Jack
Buried by a shell explosion/
clawed my way out of
a collapsed dugout
Gassed & thought I'd die/
still can't smell a thing
Mumps & Spanish influenza
& German measles & trenchfoot
Then there was
our trench companions
The dope they gave us for lice
took the skin off/
Sure it drove the lice off alright
but the cure's worse than the reason for it
Walked four miles for a bath
I took off without permission/Got the skids put under me
Caught without a permission belt around Abeele
Got into fisticuffs with an Aussie/
Got the skids put under me
I got demoted
{Please address letters to just Private again}
Most of the boys I came with are gone

But these are just the things you are willing to put in letters
Worse/perhaps far worse/was seeing what happened to others/
even the enemy/maybe especially the enemy/when it was them or you
Taking that in/That's what you'll be taking home with you in your baggage:
What you couldn't unsee/unhear/undo
The opposite of a bucket list/the list of things that happened to me

PHOTO courtesy CanadianLetters.ca

QUESTIONS ON EPITAPH NO. 67569

The gravestone suggests more questions than answers
Records show you signed up with the Chinese Labour Corps
from Shandong Province
for a few francs a week you helped win the war
Some CLC workers met ends
clearing land mines/ fired on cutting barbwire
Likely influenza brought you to hospital
in Lijssenthoek months after Armistice
perhaps while digging up/

Commonwealth bodies/
from graves dug up by shells/
to re-inter in military plots/
now the war is over
Four standard phrases on Portland stone
are set aside for CLC graves:
"Faithful unto death"
"A good reputation endures forever"
 "A noble duty bravely done"
"Though dead he still liveth"
No anglicized name here
Chinese figures/& No. 67569
identify you but records show
your name was Wang Hui Lan
& you died
6 April 1919
According to Lijssenthoek.be
your headstone means
    "gentle/gracious orchid"
    Bloomed too brief/We honour you
    "Though dead he still liveth"[40]

---

[40] PHOTO by J. Carmichael: A century later "Ensuring We Remember" @WWICLC seeks a permanent memorial the Chinese Labour Corps. 140,000 Chinese men worked for the Allied forces on the Western Front in WWI. Most worked for the British, and 40,000 for the French. Several thousand stayed in Paris after the war, most of the rest were repatriated. Five CLC workers were awarded Meritorious Service Medals, including First Class Ganger Liu Dien Chen, who rallied his men under shellfire in 1918. Zhu Guisheng, who died at 106 in 2002, also served in the French Army during World War II.

ELASTIC-BOUND NOTEBOOK

Concentrate/Focus on the future
What kind of fishing boat he'll need
What kinds of nets he'll need
Prices for salmon
Coho/Sockeye/Spring
The signals for Morse code
{those will come in handy
after the war with his work on
telegraph lines to Tofino, B.C.}
Jottings from Amiens / Scarpe
Canal du Nord / San Quentin Canal
One of the "fortunate"
marching home with this note on
Buckingham Palace letterhead
"The Queen & I wish you God-speed
and a safe return to
your homes & dear ones
A grateful Mother Country is proud
of your splendid services
characterized by unsurpassed
devotion & courage"

From the wartime photos & papers of Tofino, BC, fisherman & lifeboat worker Harold Monks, Sr
/ PHOTOS: courtesy CanadianLetters.ca / VIU

HOMEWARD BOUND

Returning wounded
the boys they once used to be
yearn for their years back

The Lord watch between thee and me when we are
parted one from another!

HOW I MET YOUR MOTHER/WAR BRIDES

For better or for worse

Hardly a place to meet a marriage prospect
Still, the Western Front was entrenched
with testosterone
For some, Blighty could be a blessing
& military hospitals — or leave
in towns away from the front
Towns with women
Towns with prospects off at war
Introductions with lasting consequence
between a patient & a nurse/
at a dance/or at church

For richer or poorer, in sickness & in health

Sometimes/in the chaos/love /
Romance in time of war had an intensity
Often buoyed by flurries of letters back & forth
Permission to marry was granted
Cpl. G. Dorman of the B.C. Regimental Depot
& Nurse B.M.G. O'Reilly/
"I am satisfied from an examination of above soldier's attestation paper
and otherwise that he is a bachelor (or widower,)" signed his CO
The bride glowing/perhaps crowned by a veil of lace
 & a pretty ankle-skimming dress/
the groom handsome in his dress kit
Norman Sydney Richards spent more than a year in hospital
where he found love & married a lovely VAD
(Volunteer Aid Detachment) nurse/
bringing her back to
Salmon Arm, B.C. In 1919

Unfortunately/Fortunately

One bit of bad luck after another turned out well for Hugh McKenzie Clark
Unfortunately conscripted away from what had been essential work – farming
Unfortunately he had to leave the family farm at Storthoaks, Saskatchewan for
basic training in Regina, then shipped to Camp Bramshott in Southern England
Unfortunately he was earmarked for service in France/ Unfortunately fate intervened
in the form of a germ: the flu pandemic swept through his regiment in August 1918 /
Fortunately by the time he recovered enough to fight, the fighting was done / Fortunately, he

transferred to Ripon in North Yorkshire, in January 1919 / Fortunately, a local girl brought him home for dinner where he met her sister Grace, a music teacher / Fortunately Hugh & Grace were married by April & the pair traveled home on the Melita / Fortunately, in Saskatchewan, Grace adapted to life on the Prairies, learning to garden, can, cook on the woodstove, & teaching piano as well / Fortunately, their granddaughter Annette Fulford, kept letters & retold their love story

To have & to hold, 'til death do us part

Sometimes a sweetheart at home waited in the wings / Back home, Alice was wooed & won by Bob Hale with notes like this one: "Please don't worry darling/I love you with all my heart and soul and I want to marry you. Remember it is for the freedom of Canada and you that we are fighting/If I go to the front and get killed, just remember me sometimes / But I think I will live to see you again ....XXXXXXXXXXXXXXXXXXXX"
And he did![41])

---

41 PHOTO courtesy Annette Fulford. According to Library & Archives Canada, an estimated 54,000 relatives and dependents accompanied troops returning to Canada through the Department of Immigration & Colonization following demobilization after World War I. With an estimated 424,000 fellows in Europe or England, and tens of thousands hospitalized with wounds, by the end of the war, Canadian soldiers were marrying British and European woman at the rate of 1,000 per month, says genealogist and war brides author Annette Fulford of Maple Ridge, BC. Thousands came in an immigrations scheme that included free third-class passage for the dependents of soldiers, paid for by the Canadian government. By August 1919, Canadian press sources estimated there were 35,000 new women immigrants. Letters/CanadianLetters.ca

HOW YOU'RE GOING TO KEEP HIM DOWN ON THE FARM

After the pounding of shells
After seeing those doing
their bit/blown to bits
After working to secure
world peace/to discover
they secured nothing
After getting a little too
used to
Service Rum Diluted
After he discovered/
absence & abstinence
& sexual health
don't always go together/
If only having seen Paree
were the biggest problem
How're you going to keep him
down on the farm? /In fact, he
will be down
on the farm
& it won't be
Because Paree

. Heroes are feted, and loved, and flattered by everyone, and some women besides professional prostitutes are tempted to throw themselves, with all that they possess, at the feet of the men returning from the wars.

There is no doubt about it, you can do anything you like with this kind of woman, and it is just here that self-control is a vital necessity.

The big man is he who can keep himself clean and pure and true in the midst of undoubtedly strong temptation.

The Hero, coming back, must say an emphatic No to such allurements of the flesh.

XXII.

THE uniform to many girls has proved a wonderful glamour, and now that you boys are returning covered with glory and honor and decorations, some of these girls who do not wish to be immoral are showing themselves free and easy in their manifestations of delight at your return.

These girls must be protected from themselves, and you men who have shown so much courage and chivalry in your strenuous and victorious opposition to the German hordes, will surely be able to act as protectors of this wonderful Canadian maidenhood.

XXIII.

Right here you should think very deeply about your attitude towards women.

Every child has a right to be well born. Furthermore, Canada has a right to expect that every child shall be well born.

This result can only come about if both the father and mother are healthy and free from Venereal Disease.

It is worthy of your best thought.

XXIV.

YOU will soon be discharged and enter civilian life once more.

You will doff your uniform and clothe yourself in the garb of former days.

Do you thereby make any change in yourself?

Not at all.

You will be just the same fellow you are now—full of life and vigor, tempted and tried, defeated or victorious.

Character is the only thing which endures forever.

Remember! Your experiences in the great war are only incidents in your career, but they will mean much in your character building.

XXV.

AS living, pulsing beings we do just four things—we work, we eat, we sleep and we play.

During the war your work has been unnatural and destructive.

XXV.

AS living, pulsing beings we do just four things—we work, we eat, we sleep and we play.

During the war your work has been unnatural and destructive.

Your eating and your sleeping have been arranged for you according to military rule.

Some of your recreation has been made according to schedule.

You are coming back to work, and eat and sleep, and play.

15

XXVII.

THE Knights of the Round Table rode forth relieving the oppressed and redressing human wrongs.

That is to be your duty during the coming years.

What have we been fighting for over there?

Well, we have been fighting for liberty and freedom and justice and righteousness, if we have been fighting for anything at all.

It was for this that more than 50,000 of our comrades are to-day lying under little white crosses in France and Flanders.

It was for this that thousands of our comrades are maimed and mutilated for life.

We surely, then, want liberty and freedom in Canada. But there can be no real freedom and no true liberty in this broad Dominion if the country is enthralled by Venereal Disease, and bound down by the fetters of immorality.

I have a fancy that the returning soldier will take a pride in the reconstruction and regeneration of Canadian society, and I have a vision of the time when Canadians of the new order will place on their standard and use as their battle cry, "Women and children first!"

XXVIII.

YOU are coming back. You are hastening just as fast as you can to the old home town, or to the farm upon the countryside, and you are anxiously looking forward to the welcome from the loved ones who have supported you by their letters and by their

17

IMAGES: Excerpts from "Coming Back"
By Fred J. Smith for the YMCA
/courtesy CanadianLetters.ca / VIU

PHOTO by J. Carmichael:
Twin graves for brothers Creighton Wellington
Hatt & F. Hatt of Marriots Cove, Nova Scotia,
both of the 25th Battalion/Canadian Infantry at
Tyne Cot Cemetery/Belgium

"In death they were not divided"
{2 Samuel 1:23}

WHERE SLEEPING GHOSTS LIE

The ghosts sleep light/
behind cool stones
attended by descendants
of those they saved a world for/or didn't
The ghosts sleep rough in the
corners of earthed-in trenches
Hunkered down under hunks of tin
shells in their midst/
raw unexploded
rifles in hand/
a sketchy slumber
fitful at an eternal Western Front
But as the Last Post echoes
their thousands of names
under silvered arches at the Menin Gate
the ghosts stand at attention
Backs rifle-straight
Spectral tears unshed at twilight[42]

---

[42] From Canada, a country of fewer than 8 million souls, some 619,636 Canadians
enlisted in the Canadian Expeditionary Force. 59,544 died. Almost three times that many were wounded.

PHOTO by J. Carmichael: Bronze statue by T.J. Clapperton of a soldier consoling a boy, who represents humanity, at the World War I memorial in Oamaru, New Zealand. Memorial designed by E. Miller & unveiled ANZAC day 1926. Quote by Rudyard Kipling "From little towns in a far land we came to save our honour and a world aflame; by little towns, in a far land, we sleep and trust those things we won to you to keep."

#LONG AFTER

Family snapshot of George "Black Jack" Vowel, third from left, with his parents
Caloway & Ellen Vowel, and children Margaret (Peggy), Jacqueline, Barbara and John.

BLACK JACK/MORE GUTS THAN A SLAUGHTERHOUSE

Armistice You underline the date*:* *11 November 1918*
A single entry in your journal: *'returned boots'*
After finally occupying Germany
{& *really* enjoying Cologne}
discharged 5 May 1919 in Toronto
You snap your war journal shut after writing:
"arrived home today/finished with the army
after 4 years nine months absence"
Son Don will volunteer for World War II
Son Jack/to his bitter disappointment won't go off to war/
ruled 4F between poor vision & childhood rickets
An older soldier Don meets in the war in Europe
tells him about you "Black Jack"
"There was never a better soldier ever lived"
That you weren't afraid of anything
That you had "more guts than a slaughterhouse"
{Your letters from the slaughterhouse of the Western Front suggest different} /*The Somme / Vimy /*
Festubert / Cambrai / St. Eloi /Mount Sorrel / Passchendaele Kitcheners Wood /St. Julien / Thiepval /
Albert / Arras / etc
A hundred years after the war when the woman at the Enterprise counter in Amsterdam
{on learning I am Canadian} smiles broadly & says "You rescued us! Twice!"
I just smile & tell her for you: She's welcome

THREE MEDALS FOR VALOUR / AND LIVING TO TELL

Immigrated from Britain to Edmonton, Alberta at 14,
enrolled at The University of Alberta
when World War I broke out,

Capt. George Burdon McKean
enlisted with the Canadian Expeditionary Force
One of very few who won
three separate medals
for outstanding valour
& lived to tell about it
First it was the Military Medal for
rescuing wounded men under fire in 1917
Then, as a lieutenant with
the Royal Montreal Regiment,
he was given the Victoria Cross
for leaping headfirst
into a group of Germans,
single-handedly gaining
the upper hand/killing some

taking others captive,
and destroying a dugout
The Military Cross at Cagnicourt
for incredible bravery in
Canada's "Hundred Days"
near the close of the war in Arras.
His book, "Scouting Thrills: The Memoir
of a Scout Officer in the Great War"
released in 1919 (re-issued in 2003)
He re-upped with the Army, leaving in 1926
But then/
stopped in his tracks
by an industrial accident
Just as a new life was beginning

Alas, destiny took a tragic hand: all those medals, but a regular job turned out to be the most dangerous thing.
George Burdon McKean was killed in a freak industrial accident in England in 1926 when a circular saw blade
came loose, striking him in the head. Two days later, his widow bore him a baby daughter. George Burdon
McKean's Victoria Cross is on display at the War Museum of Canada. Photo/Public Domain

BLACK JACK/PTSD/WHAT HAPPENED

{Post}
Not many of the original Tenth Battalion left
Lost more of the boys in Festubert on 21 May
I came through alright but words cannot describe
the scenes we went through at Ypres were >

{Traumatic}
I often wonder how any of us made it through
We fought six days/four days without food
Some of the boys got no sleep for almost a week
What does that leave you with? >

{Stress}
Slows the pulse to near zero
Wills the heart to stop pumping
Turns you from man to stone
& from rational thought to psychic >

{Disorder}
If / when they get home
We will win the war in time
but at what personal cost?
It will be many decades before the term PTSD is coined
{How many of them have it?}

The "Great War for Civilisation"
Now that's a crock/some wonder
How could something so uncivilized
How could something that lays waste an entire generation
Something that uses so many shells to reduce men to shells
How could that ever be great? [43]

---

[43] Victory Medal, flip side, issued to George Anderson "Black Jack" Vowel

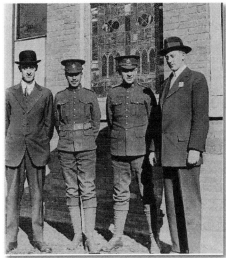

ONE SOLDIER'S WAR - Robert Shortreed (seen above at a falls with a straw boater hat) went home to Guelph to sign up for WWI on 6 Nov 1916. Right, at enlistment. Below, his 2nd Canadian Siege Battery marching drill. PHOTOS/LETTERS CanadianLetters.ca/VIU

ONE SOLDIER'S WAR

In 1975 - Like one of those celeb photos that
morphs year by year/
from young to old/
the photos from the collection
of Robert Shortreed/
photos that articulate a world about world war
without a word/
chronicling a most hideous war/
in a most unusual century/

& the technology rocketing us into this one
If Robert Shortreed was like us {just demonstrably braver perhaps}
Did he wonder "How did I get here from there?"
In a few short blinks — perhaps terrifyingly long during the war
— from strong, clear-eyed youth/ to seasoned, distinguished veteran/In 1975
We read into the lines/the glasses/the silver hair/the cane
We behold the enduring brotherhood of any who suffer a thing together
& perhaps that life cradle-to-grave rushes by for us all & so — {respect}

PHOTO LEFT: Robert Shortreed
of Guelph, Ontario was a
salesman who enlisted with the
64th Depot Batt. of the Canadian
Field Artillery, at a reunion of the
2nd Canadian Siege
Battery/Charlottetown PEI 1975

TOP PHOTO: Shortreed's 2nd Canadian Siege Battery in action at Canal-du-Nord, France 27 Sept 1918.
CanadianLetters.ca / VIU

HARRY PATCH/THE LAST SURVIVING WWI SOLDIER

No guns allowed at the funeral of the Last Tommy
Not even a service weapon/Not a one
Plenty of questions from
the last surviving soldier of the Western Front
Harry Patch wanted to know:
What's logical about a licence to go out & murder/
to commit "calculated & condoned slaughter of human beings"?
Why shoot a man you never knew?
Why kill a bloke you never had a quarrel with?
If you couldn't even speak his language/why address him with a gun?
"All those lives lost for a war finished over a table"
What's the sense in that? Harry Patch wanted to know[44]

---

[44] PHOTO by Stephen Kerr: Contalmaison The Second Canadian Cemetery and the Sunken Road Cemetery, amidst French farmland.

Harry Patch, "The Last Fighting Tommy," was the last surviving combat soldier of the First World War. He died in 2009 at age 111 years, 1 month, 1 week, and one day. A native of Combe Down, Somerset, England, Patch was injured at Passchendaele on 22 Sept 1917.

SONGS OF WWI

Pack Up the Troubles of Your Old Kit Bag
& smile/smile/smile
Johnny
The pipes/the pipes are calling
because It's a Long Way to Tipperary
& you will resent being down on the farm
After You've Seen Paree
{if you make it home at all}
When Johnny Comes Marching Home
{if you can still march then} we'll
Keep The Homefires Burning {the house down}

Four years of fighting /Johnny
& you went from every
corner of the country
{of every country}
from the colony of Newfoundland
from the States
to London/to Ypres/to Vimy/to Cologne
From charming & witty
to brusque & withdrawn
From clever repartee
to stone-faced
to weeping/to sullen
to morose/to bellowing
We can't imagine what makes you
so difficult to live with/
Johnny
Is it because   we can't imagine?

The 1914-1915 Medal awarded to George Anderson "Black Jack" Vowel & over 70,000 other CEF soldiers. Photo courtesy Brian Vowel.

WWI WIFE'S TALE/HELL/THE CONQUERING HERO

I was engaged to a boy who didn't return from the war
Then I met my husband
Wooed by his intensity/ his deep-set blue eyes haunted
& somehow vulnerable & vivid
Someone looks at you that intently
   -     positively cross-eyed with attention
You think you know what it means
You think it means love & patience & understanding & closeness
His thick dark hair luxuriant under my fingers/
His muscled frame
His farming background

& he looked so good in uniform
We had so much in common {I thought}
I was quiet/he was quiet
but I didn't know   why he was quiet
I didn't know about the battery of images
flickering behind his eyelids/
that war was both the making of him/
and his undoing
As I put my hair up for our wedding
I dreamed of a family
Our wedding notice in the paper
was all "happy Mr & Mrs"
& "honeymooning in Idaho"
The children came soon enough
The first/a boy/blond curls tousled
bright eyes merry
But fatherhood was another kind of trench/He teased the
child mercilessly
Excluding him for the slightest offense/
engaging the boy in battle
I was wary but hapless / I begged for fatherly
compassion/for truce /
I was as compassionate as I could be

PHOTO: Young John Vowel astride a plow horse at the farm in Hotchkiss, Alberta, early 1920s — family photo

Walking on eggshells/
blaming myself
I could hardly blame the war
as he would never talk about it
but I came to know his damage
More children quickly followed
& the Depression on their heels/
little paid work/little food/
no money but unlimited bitterness
His taste for booze/nurtured for years in the trenches
Made him itchy with a misery unscratchable
His wrath a pit/a dugout/a shell-hole
with iron stakes/at the bottom
From high hopes/to last hopes/
to no hopes/I put up with the tumult
Endured the chaos
Tried to get the kids to be good/to be quiet
But when the last of them were safely out of school /
I left him because sometimes love is not enough &
because there was no language
for what dogged him/
No therapy/No diagnosis/No treatment

When he died I shed my tears at a distance/
tears for him/for me/for my son/
scarred by his father's searing disinterest
That son went on to drink heavily/
roar at his own children
Tears for all the men/
for all the sons & daughters cut down for generations
An eternal onslaught of emotions
A phantom war never really quite over[45]

---

[45] Genealogist/researcher Annette Fulford has interviewed hundreds of descendants of war brides for her blog and an upcoming book on war brides. PTSD played a role in the disintegration of some of the unions of the returning soldiers, she said. "There were some returning soldiers who couldn't deal with life - and a few brides who had to get rescued by their parents," Fulford said.

PHOTO: Laura & George "Black Jack" Vowel, family photo

WORD ASSOCIATION GAME

Rifle stock/Shell-shocked
Flares/Scared
Barrage/Damaged
Cauterized/Traumatized
Shard/Scarred
Shelling abated/Unrehabilitated
Arriving/Surviving
Service/Sacrifice
Post Traumatic Stress Disorder[46]

---

[46] "... the crying, fear, paralysis, or insanity of soldiers exposed to the stress and horror of the trenches was often held by medical professionals to be the result of physical damage to the brain by the shock of exploding shells. Military authorities often saw its symptoms as expressions of cowardice or lack of moral character." — www.WarMuseum.ca

PHOTO by Geerhard Joos PHOTO ILLUSTRATION: Brad K. Larson

TWO ROADS DIVERGE IN SANCTUARY WOOD

Two Members of Parliament/Two Lieutenant Colonels/Two distinguished in battle
Two die in World War I {while sitting in Canadian Parliament}

{dying in Flanders while sitting in Parliament}
One Lt.-Col. George Harold Baker, 38/
MP for Brome Quebec /
dies at Mt. Sorrel/at Sanctuary Wood
on the Ypres Salient 2 Jun 1916
& they put up a bronze statue
in Parliament

The other/Lt. Col. Samuel Simpson Sharpe, 45
MP for Ontario North/ re-elected in absentia while overseas
by twice as many votes as his opponent
Sharpe leads his battalion into battle at
Vimy Ridge/Hill 70/Passchendaele/sees hundreds of his men die
While being treated for nervous shock/Sharpe dies 25 May 1918
jumping from the window of the Royal Victoria Hospital
"He gave up his life as truly 'on the field of honour' as if he had fallen in action"
-   {Stewart Lyon/The Toronto Globe 27 May 1918}
Parliament turns the blind eye of silent men
To be fair/to this day
few know what to say or do about suicide {one of the last taboos}
Samuel Simpson Sharpe's service would be basically
ignored in Ottawa for almost a century[47]

The Cromlech memorial in Welsh National Memorial Park, Langemark, Belgium. The red dragon honours soldiers of Welsh descent, and those attached to Welsh divisions. The stones were brought from Wales, the bronze was designed by Lee Odishow, and the memorial was designed by Erwin Ureel

[47] A full century after Sam Sharpe's death, a sculpted plaque of him is installed at Parliament, the creation of sculptor Tyler Briley, a former first responder with PTSD. An annual Sam Sharpe Breakfast in Ottawa now helps MPs learn more about mental wellness issues amongst service members and veterans. Sam Sharpe Breakfast co-founder {with Gen. Romeo Dallaire} Erin O'Toole, MP for Durham, Ontario said, "Parliament recognizes that service in uniform can lead to both physical and mental wounds. Parliament can send a clear signal of support to people suffering with mental health issues by righting this wrong."

According to the Lucy Maud Montgomery page at ConfederationCentre.com, Canada's beloved author of the Anne of Green Gables series, lived in Sharpe's riding, was socially acquainted with his wife, Mabel. Clippings show she followed Sharpe's 116th Battalion. A sad note in Montgomery's journal: "We went to Uxbridge this afternoon to see a military funeral. Colonel Sam Sharpe, for whom I voted last December was buried. He came home from the front quite recently, insane from shell-shock and jumped from a window in the Royal Victoria in Montreal. Thousands of people attended the funeral."

Vowel Family Fishing Trip/circa 1930

WHY IS HIS OWN FIRST SON AFRAID OF HIM?

Why is his own first son afraid of him?
Why should the boy cringe in the corner hiding tears behind blond curls
as if Father sent him there/as if a stern manner meant he doesn't love the child
When he doesn't spare the rod/ why should he take the kid fishing?
Why shouldn't he bellow ? Life is hard/the rations few/
the guns in the distance almost as loud to him
now in a way/with peace looming around as they ever were on the Western Front
The buzz in his own head keener still/now to him than anything other sound
He was never a boy like his son
No, he was his father's ranch hand
Father applied the iron of his will
So he will cobble his own first son's worn shoes with cardboard
& when the boy is muscled & ready for harness/
he can quit school/help on the farm
Surely no more hardship than they faced in the trenches of the Great War
Why is his own first son afraid of him?
{& will his son's daughter be afraid of her father?}
{How many generations of a family can the parasite of war work its way through?}

DNA

"There has been such a focus on veterans and PTSD in the media, which is great, but somehow
the missing piece is how that PTSD also affects a person's family."
Christal Presley, author of *Finding Peace from Wartime PTSD*
on CNN on 25 April 2017

A soldier's granddaughter
feels the strands/the
DNA inside
of her
cells
the coded
messages twisting,
alive to her blood/the danger
of the trenches/the threat of
the enemy/He bellowed
at his son & his son
bellowed at the
grandbaby
so loud
she
tumbled
off the couch
He was a mean drunk/
Funny first/then mean
& his son was too
She avoids
drink
to
pre-empt
any problems &
hopes it's enough &
she wonders & she worries
will she bellow/who they
will bellow at & if
bellowing is
the worst
of it
& if the
impact will ever
cease this generation

IT TOLLS FOR THEE

Ringing/ still ringing*
in my ears war ringing / Father*
is proud & stern on the platform/Mother is*
weeping quietly/I hear her so loud & clear over the*
urgent clang at the train station/going/going/going*
going/going/High piercing mosquito tone ever—present/the*
wee gift of shell explosions/never fades/A maniac devil fiddles in*
between my ears / scarred church steeple / enwreathed with chimes*
of armistice/**My helmet is the bell & i am the clapper** /gone /gone/gone/gone*
Inside of me a scared kid / Inside of me the cry of a wolf / a ringing / a roaring*

Will it*
never ever*
ever ever*
hush?*

PHOTO by Nick Mol/Fotoshoot WO1oo: Cobbers sculpture of Sergeant Simon Fraser of the 57th Battalion AIF, by Peter Corlett at VC Corner Cemetery, Australian Memorial Park at the site of The Battle of Fromelles (19-21 July 1916). Fraser was one of many who went back to the scene of the battle to retrieve wounded men from the 60th Battalion. He was later killed at Bullecourt 11-12 May 1917.

ANOTHER CHAOS

When his buddies come for a visit/old friends or the few left after the chaos of war
the few who know what the chaos was/the ~~good old~~ bad-old days in the trenches
{the boys they left under headstones or buried by shells who knows where}
They sit at the lake/Catch fish or not/Drink beer
Let things slide a little/
Let other things percolate
Chaos now is six kids need new shoes
A trench now is in lieu of regular dental care/
the Wife needs new teeth
The battle now is with drought
The skirmish now is the price per ton of grain/
He'll be damned if those kids will have it easier than the poor devils
who never made it home after giving it their full measure
The war is ended/The battle begins
Gone/fishing
No/son/
You can't go fishing with us
Don't ask again

TOP: with buddies, George Anderson "Black Jack" Vowel/decades after spending 1914-1919 in World War I &
on the Western Front.
PHOTO ILLUSTRATION: Brad K. Larson /family photo courtesy Brian Vowel

World War I veteran Charles Wellington Camden Chapman receives a medal from his friend Tommy Douglas MP / often considered Canada's most important citizen PHOTO: Family

THE OTHER GRANDFATHER

Charles Wellington Camden Chapman
Saskatchewan rancher/cowboy son
of an Anglican minister/adventurer
Raised partly in Fort Churchill
Four long years at war
{& another six months occupying Germany}
as an artillery man/operating a gun that
lobbed 18-pound shells at Fritz
Wounded 13 Oct 1915 in the leg
& shrapnel from
a nearby shell imbedded in his back/
hospitalized 69 days from 1915-1916
Subjected to poison gas
After four long years at war/
despite an obvious wound
he came home whole far as you could tell/
A bit of a limp & a bit hard of hearing
{every so often he'd go to the veterans'
hospital & they'd take another out}
Kind blue eyes crinkled at the corners
a hearty laugh that rattled in a chest damaged
by mustard gas in the Great War
"Rancher returns to Canada"

Married a lovely Canadian girl of global roots
- French & German stock -
He & Ruth raised six children
North Battleford was a Dust Bowl bust
in the Depression so he sold the farm
for the price of a used car & a few bucks
& he loaded up the clan with suitcases tied
to the running boards

& mattresses strapped on top
& came to Ladysmith/Nanaimo
/Port Alberni
to work as a foreman
at the chipper plant at
Bloedel Stewart & Welchl
& my Uncle Charlie says
when Grandpa's kids asked him if he
killed any Germans in the war he
grinned & said
he only practiced on
bully beef tins
Even after four long years at war he
wanted to volunteer for World War II
Told he was too old to enlist
he served in the home militia
Not a perfect life/
but a genuinely nice guy
Cheerful/kind/nurturing Beloved by his
children & grandchildren
Outlived three wives/but not his sense
of humour
Bore his decline gracefully
Played a mean harmonica with dignity
in the kitchen band at the seniors home
in Parksville
I descend from two World War I
veterans
For one/WWI was the making of him
For another/WWI was

the making of him & the breaking of him/& almost the end of him
& I wonder about the differences in their lives
What is between the threads of their wartime experiences
that I don't know about?

In the wartime memoir "Private Peat," author & war hero Harold Peat captioned this photo "Are we downhearted?" A common cheer often met with a rousing "No!"

QUESTIONS/FROM A 1936 MEMOIR BY CHARLES H. SAVAGE

Some enlisted for adventure, or because they were fed up and wanted a change; while the fear of being thought afraid probably influenced many
The great majority of us enlisted because we felt that whether we liked it or not
   — we were committed to a great war, & that other men
were being killed doing a job that was as much our duty as theirs ...
... Like most soldiers, he left the hating of the enemy to non-combatants.
Of course we cursed the Germans & called them all manner of foul names;
but we did the same to our friends, much worse to those
whom we disliked on our own side
Most of those whom we killed we didn't hate:
in fact we often had a decided feeling of respect for them
If in peace time a man does me great wrong & I kill him, I am a murderer;
the state takes my life in punishment
In war I kill a man whom I do not hate, in fact whom I may respect,
a man who has probably never harmed me in any way;
I am a hero, the state pays me for doing it
This does not sound right: let us start again ...
Germany violated the neutrality of Belgium; therefore she must be punished;

therefore I must proceed to kill as many Germans as I possibly can;
Most of these Germans knew nothing of any violated neutrality,

or were convinced that necessity justified the
action /I am acting as accuser, jury, judge &
executioner, or my country is
This hardly seems right
If I suspected a man of murder/
I should hardly go out & shoot him
I should turn him over to the officers of justice
They might be obliged to kill him
but it would be done legally ...
... We know that there is something wrong in a
system that makes us kill those whom as
individuals we do not hate and who individually
do not hate or even dislike us
... We are not pacifists.
If our country becomes involved in war, we will
fight, and fight hard, but we shall do it much
more willingly if we know that our rulers and
leaders have done everything in their power
to bring about a state where war is impossible...
With most of us such thoughts
were put aside until after the war

Once in it there was
but one safe philosophy,
and we said to ourselves,
'Right or wrong we are now
in a fight for our very existence;
we must think of one thing only,
winning.
Each encounter
is a game
with the high stake
of life or death'"[48]

---

[48] Charles Henry Savage of Eastman, Quebec, enlisted at Sherbrooke in February 1915 with the 5th Canadian Mounted Rifles. He wrote a memoir of World War I in 1936. He died in Montreal at age 85. PHOTO, complete memoir online courtesy CanadianLetters.ca / VIU

ARCHES

Hush
These arches ring,
hallowed
Ad Majorem Dei Gloriam
Every evening at 8 p.m. precisely
Here are recorded names of officers and men
the mournful trumpet of the Last Post
who fell in Ypres Salient
echoes round/Heads bow/voices fall silent
Thousands stand quiet for the sacred moment
but to whom the fortune of war
Remembering war's profanity
denied the known and honoured burial
in rain, snow or bitterest cold
given to their comrades in death
We don't know where they are
but we know where to find their names
Hush[49]

---

[49] PHOTO by J. Carmichael: Unveiled 24 July 1927, the Menin Gate in Ieper bears 54,896 names of Commonwealth soldiers missing in action before August 15, 1917. It was designed by Sir Reginald Blomfeld. Bold text from memorial

TYNE COT

Rounded meadow
"In the course of my pilgrimage,
I have many times
asked myself
crisp in the sun's rays
on a chill November day
whether there can be
more potent advocates
these tranquil
sweeping lines with
11,965 buried beneath
stark white grave stones
of peace upon Earth
through the years to come
than this
The largest
Commonwealth cemetery
from any war   ever
Carved into these curved walls
34,997 names
massed multitude of silent witnesses
to the desolation of war"
— King George V, 11 May 1922
Each letter precision set
We don't know where they are
but we know where
to find their names[50]

---

[50] Tyne Cot's curved wall is the repository of 34,997 names of Commonwealth soldiers MIA between August 1917 & November 1918 . Tyne Cot designed by Sir Herbert Baker, with sculptures by Joseph Armitage and Ferdinand Victor Blundstone. Blundstone designed the Newfoundland Memorial.

PHOTO by J. Carmichael/photo illustration Brad K. Larson: High school students visit Tyne Cot cemetery, the largest Commonwealth soldiers cemetery. Bold text from the speech of King George at Tyne Cot.

AROUND US

Ring of Remembrance
on the hills
of the Artois/
Around us
Just 600,000 names of
soldiers who fell
now the largest military
cemetery
in France
Notre-Dame-de-
Lorette International
Memorial at
Ablain-St-Nazaire/
Nord Pas de Calais
No distinction
by nationality
No regard for gender
No barriers of religion
A century on/
an echo of
much-needed
universal perspective
in Philippe Prost's
design
Around us
Just humans
remembering/
remembered
together
A cloud
of witnesses
Around us

Photo by Stephen Kerr/SK Photography

PHOTO by Kevin Raistrick: New Zealanders perform a commemorative Haka at the Menin Gate on July 18, 2018. Around 18,000 New Zealanders died in WWI.

DIGGING HISTORY

I.   Up pops an ulna: bones are discovered every month/still
Each time the police have to come inspect some small fragment to make sure
they really date to the Great War era/not some hapless modern crime victim
A specialist checks to see if a German boot/Commonwealth button/ fragment of leather from an

ANZAC hat/ thread from a Turkish colonial's
garb/ rusted-out sidearm or some other
artifact can place the tissue fragment with
one side or another for burial purposes &
perhaps even to weave into some episode of
War Junk WWI
on the History Channel
All over the former Western Front/now mild
with homes & flowers & fields still dimpled
with crater lines & creased with trenches
unexploded ordnance
secreted over time/
Dig very, very carefully

PHOTO by Steve Van Den Eynde:/ A harvest of ancient WWI bombs unearthed on the Western Front

II.   Usually as an occupation
But typically for the sheer passion of helping people learn about war/
professional guides
visit to/take photos of
post about/
guide around/
research/illuminate
memorials & landmarks & graves
dug a century ago
Modern shepherds
helping people
excavate their personal pasts

Museum curators at the Auckland War Memorial Museum present touching films of 1918 with hakas of welcome & of grief & the next generation of poets around New Zealand/ recalling the sacrifices of their ANZACs forefathers

Belgian photographer Geerhard Joos has captured the Vimy Memorial in every possible light/Visually chronicling families who lost more than one son to WWI/But his specialty is the SAD — Shot At Dawns/ travelling the world to capture their headstones / "I felt a lot of these guys were done a great injustice ... So my sense of justice told me to treat them with equal respect, and I take their photos as well," he says

TOP PHOTO by Nick Mol/Fotoshoot WO1oo: Guide Gérard Brusco at La Tranchée de Chattancourt redug at the location of an active French WWI frontline trench at Verdun, rebuilt to specs according to original maps and photos and soldier accounts of 1916.

ABOVE PHOTO courtesy Steve Douglas: Salient Tours staff with Steve Douglas, far left, at the gravesite of Lt. Col. Dr. John McCrae, trench doctor/poet who wrote "In Flanders Fields"

III.   British Author Lucy London commemorates fascinating
& often long-forgotten people
 involved in the conflict at
femalewarpoets.blogspot.com
Her exhibit on female poets for a 2012 exhibition
at The Wilfred Owen Story museum in Birkenhead/Wirral/
led to books/weblogs/Facebook pages/
filled with fascinating facts & heart-touching stories /
Like the discovery of canine film star Rin Tin Tin
by an American Doughboy in Alsace

Social media savvy/100 years later/
Centenary upon centenary/
Facebook pages spring up/dedicated to a history &
a heroism almost obliterated by the fracking of time
They highlight the work of researchers
Interest a new generation in the travails &

trails & trials & losses & discoveries of bygone generations/
finding fresh perspective on the impact of a 'Great' War
These new explorers with their own "tweets from the trenches"
call for some new kind of recognition/
not 'like' or 'heart' or 'sad face'/
Perhaps 'respect face' or 'fascinated' face/
Perhaps a poppy emoji/as with brave new tools/
with digital shovels we   down   history
                          dig   into

PHOTO LEFT: by J. Carmichael: Battlefield guide Raoul Saesen
helps a client look up a Commonwealth soldier on an interactive
display at In Flanders Fields Museum in Ieper

PHOTO RIGHT: tattoos on the arm of Steven Van Den Eynde, a
Belgium resident who honors the memory of several soldiers who
died in WWI. Art by Mariska Van Lissum, Cirk Tattoo/Aalst

WITH APOLOGIES TO LT. COL. DR. JOHN McCRAE

A hundred years later
the larks still bravely sing/fly
but all's never silent
from guns somewhere on this globe
We live this hectic century
We wear the Legion poppy to show
we've not forgotten
the waste of life long years ago/
That brave people lived/loved
served/died in Flanders Fields
& brave people still live/love/serve/die
We wear the Legion poppy to show
your words live on long after you
We wear the Legion poppy to show
that though this old world
has indeed broken faith
with you who've died
we support those who serve
in any generation
We wear the Legion poppy to show
we hope you'll rest in peace
amidst the poppies
In Flanders Fields

PHOTOS by J. Carmichael/ photo
illustrations by Brad Larson: TOP: A
visitor walks near the field station where
"In Flanders Fields" poet
Lt. Col. Dr. John McCrae
operated at Essex Farm.

ACKNOWLEDGMENTS

Ongoing sincere appreciation for the amazing work of Dr. Stephen Davies & his crew at Vancouver Island University's CanadianLetters.ca. Technical gratitude to computer guru Brad K. Larson with his fine work. Thanks to editors, newspapers & publications that welcomed my articles about Black Jack and the Western Front, like The Edmonton Sun, The Toronto Sun, The Peace River Record Gazette, The Hanna Herald, The Alberni Valley News, The Halifax Chronicle Herald, Alberta Views magazine, The Quad Cities Times. Gratitude to Steven Van Den Eynde for his breathtaking cover photo of Canada Bereft at Vimy. I find myself indebted to the keepers of history's flames, organizations like VisitFlanders, the Citadel Museum in Halifax, Ontario Government Archives, Canadian War Museum in Ottawa, The National Library & Archive, the National World War I Museum & Memorial in Kansas City, Missouri, the Auckland War Memorial Museum in New Zealand, the Canadian National Vimy Memorial, the Ellis County Museum in Waxahachie, Texas, In Flanders Fields museum at Ieper, Belgium, VisitFlanders, MMP17 Passchendaele museum in Zonnebeke, Belgium, Talbot House museum in Poperinge, Belgium, Lijssenthoek museum in Belgium, the Red Star Line Museum in Antwerp, the British Grenadier Bookshop in Ieper, Fields of Gold B&B in Ieper. Collaborative appreciation goes to Gerry Carmichael, Island Blue Printing, Lisa Kaminski at Sitezeal, Yvonne Blomer, Cynthia Sharp, Grace Vermeer, Dr. Lindsey Carmichael, Rod Bartlett, Bill Irving, Milton Hinnant, Betty Tryon, Patty Sralla, Chris & Jo Bhore, Ann Graham Walker, Candice James, Autumn Phillips, Brenda Riojas, Neal White, Brian Vowel, Carol Aston, Marc & Patricia Betournay, Craig Shemilt, Mark Leiren-Young, D.S. Stymeist, Susan Lee of Blackberry Cove Marketplace Bookstore in Ucluelet, B.C., Jeremy Loome, Rod Bartlett, Kendall Larson, Chris & Susan Baker. Historical appreciation is due Nick Mol of Fotoshoot WO1oo, Andrew Mackay, Johan Declef, Daphne Vangheluwe, Richard Houghton, Lies Depuydt, Raoul Saesen, Paul Chapman, Lucy London, Annette Fulford, Steve Douglas, Kevin Raistrick, Geerhard Joos, Nora Platt, Stephen Kerr, Ian Fletcher, Ginger Stevens Monette, Andy Wright, Peter Kervarec, Mariska Van Lissum, Sanchari Pal, Mindelle Jacobs, Stephen Novik. Thanks to my early readers, including Autumn Phillips, Gord Johns MP, Graham Thomson, Maj. (Ret.) Ken Hynes, Derek Hanebury, Susan Stenson, Jude Neale, Gary Poignant, Christina Myers, Theresa Tag Goulet, Connie Stevens, Susie Quinn, Parker Hogan, Marc & Patricia Betournay, Bill Chapman, to my advanced readers, and the writing communities at Simon Fraser University's The Writers Studio, particularly the Fictionistas - Emily Olsen, Coranne Creswell, Jennifer Fayloga Santucci, Liz Laidlaw & Sandy Ilsley, to Wayde Compton, June Hutton, Paul Headrick; the Federation of BC Writers, Haiku Canada, Planet Earth Poetry in Victoria, Words on Fire of the Alberni Valley & Char's Landing, Royal City Literary Arts Society, Poetic Justice of New Westminster, The Dominion Reading Series, 15 Minutes of Infamy in Nanaimo. And finally, familial military appreciation goes to Korean War veteran Stanley Carmichael, RCAF Warrant Officer Charles Chapman, Mary Jane Green, John Hargrove, WWII veteran Donald Vowel, Charles W.C. Chapman, Pte. Roger Irving, Fred Everard. And of course, George "Black Jack" Vowel for your words, and always, the brave men & women whose little true stories can be found in this book, and in the hearts of those who remember.

ABOUT THE AUTHOR

The granddaughter of two men who were soldiers in World War I for the duration of it, Jacqueline Larson Carmichael is a poet, working on a novel, who has made a career of journalism. Her work has appeared in news, travel & opinion articles in publications as diverse as The Dallas Morning News, Entrepreneur Magazine, The Alberni Valley News, The Westerly News, and the Toronto Sun.

She taught journalism to young people in the gifted program at University of Texas Rio Grande Valley in Texas and at the Alberta Legislature. She is a recipient of the Texas Associated Press Managing Editors First Place Award for feature series writing. Her travel articles about Flanders have appeared in several publications. She co-authored The FabJob Guide to Become a Party Planner. The dual American-Canadian citizen attended Assiniboine Community College, and Simon Fraser University's Writers Studio fiction program. She lives on Vancouver Island, British Columbia, with her family and two noisy Shetland sheepdogs.

A MESSAGE FROM THE AUTHOR:

Thank you for your interest in the Little True Stories from the Western Front to be found in Tweets from the Trenches. If you appreciate this little volume, it would mean a great deal to me if you would post a review on Amazon or GoodReads. Look up "Tweets from the Trenches" and let us know what you honestly thought about the book. This gesture would be amazing. You can also reach out via email to carmichael.jacqueline@gmail.com.

I would like to invite you to like "Tweets from the Trenches: Little True Stories of Life & Death on the Western Front" on Facebook, and to check tweetsfromthetrenches.com for more stories and photos and links to fascinating resources, including a curriculum guide with practical classroom ideas for teachers.

It's my sincere hope the little true stories in this project combining history, poetry & journalism will have something for everyone who appreciates any of those things.
Kind regards,

JACQUELINE CARMICHAEL

MORE PRAISE FOR
'TWEETS FROM THE TRENCHES'

A COMPELLING JOURNEY

'A brilliant and beautiful gift from Jacqueline Carmichael to her grandfather and everyone who picks up this remarkable book. The compelling journey is both educational and riveting, often at the same time ... This book is indeed worth retweeting.'
– GARY POIGNANT,
THE NELSON STAR

'A PROFOUND ARCHIVAL WORK THAT WILL RESONATE WITH ALL CANADIANS'

'Unlike McCrae's larks still bravely singing, Carmichael's characters are definitely heard among the guns below ... Jacqueline's creative fieldwork combined with personal letters forges a profound archival work that will resonate with all Canadians.'
– SUSAN STENSON, AUTHOR OF 'NOBODY MOVE'

'GORGEOUSLY DESIGNED, ENGAGING & DYNAMIC'

'In this wildly creative book, respected journalist J.L. Carmichael brings the reality of world war to a generation raised on reality TV and social media. Gorgeously designed, engaging, and dynamic, *TWEETS FROM THE TRENCHES* makes real the sacrifices of young people in WWI. Highly recommended for readers of all ages.'
– THERESA TAG GOULET, FOUNDER/FAB JOB PUBLISHING

'HISTORY ENDURING'

'Carmichael melds today's smartphone technology and methods of communication with the importance of yesterday's stories ... Photos and memorabilia from her own journey to the Western Front act like screenshots, capturing what for soldiers were fleeting moments, and to the rest of us are history enduring.'
– SUSIE QUINN, EDITOR/ALBERNI VALLEY NEWS

'AN IMPORTANT READ'

'Tweets from the Trenches' is an excellent classroom resource for any Canadian teacher or high school student looking to bring the human experience of World War I to light in a whole and comprehensive manner, complete with direct quotes from the men and women who lived near the front lines. As a journalist, Carmichael is not afraid to look for the whole truth of the intergenerational effects of the trauma of war, as it steals lives like a coiled serpent springing on new prey through decades. On the centennial of the peace armistice, this is an important read ... and a strong resource for both language arts and socials students in high schools and colleges. Carmichael reminds us that poetry can be meaningful and heartfelt while still being readily accessible.'
— CYNTHIA SHARP, AUTHOR/'RAINFOREST IN RUSSET'

'LYRICAL EXPLORATION OF FORM & LANGUAGE'

'By permitting glimpses into a host of very human lives, loves, tragedies and victories, author Jacqueline Carmichael delivers a touching and intimate book that is both accessible and challenging. With a beautiful and at times startling blend of the visual and the literary — including prose, poetry, photos and more — Tweets From the Trenches is equal parts historical journalism and narrative non-fiction family memoir. This lyrical exploration of form and language is a treat to read, and a timely reminder of the humanity of those who have come before.'
— CHRISTINA MYERS, BLOGGER, CO-FOUNDER/WORDS IN THE BURBS

'FASCINATING READ!'

'What a fascinating read! ... it's thorough, informative, eye opening and should be required reading in a college or high school history course.'
— CONNIE STEVENS, ACTOR/DIRECTOR/PRODUCER

'HAUNTING REALITY ... BROUGHT INTO SHARP FOCUS'

'The haunting reality of war fought more than a century ago is brought into sharp focus presently in Jacqueline Carmichael's presentation of writing from the front lines by those that lived it and died by it.'
— PARKER HOGAN, PRINCIPAL/THE HOGAN GROUP

'POIGNANTLY SPEAKS'

'Jackie Carmichael ... helps bring history to life and makes it readily accessible to young readers. A thread that runs through the entire book is that soldiers were and are real people, with hopes, dreams and aspirations. Tens of thousands of those soldiers never got to live out their dreams. Carmichael's work poignantly speaks for those whose voices have been silent for one hundred years.'
— Maj. (Ret.) KEN HYNES, CHIEF CURATOR/THE ARMY MUSEUM HALIFAX CITADEL

Printed in Great Britain
by Amazon